An Unforgettable Pastime

By

Michael Anthony Vitale

DEDICATION

This book's dedication is to God Almighty, Mom and Dad.

Without whom, I could not have authored this book.

Without them, this book would not have been.

(SCORECARD)

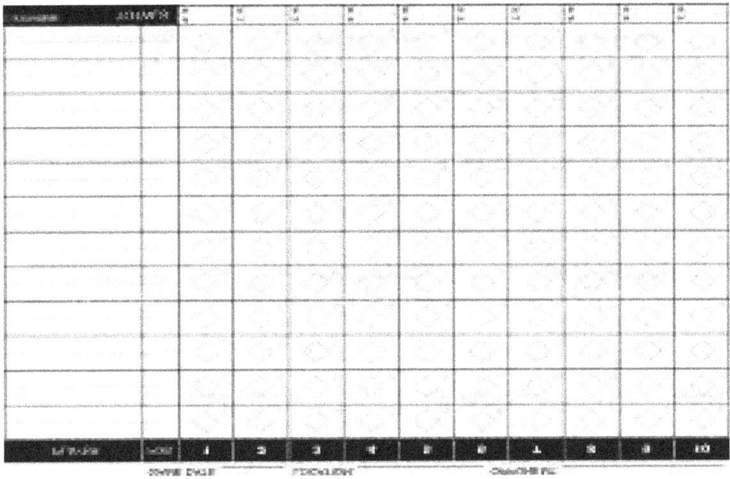

Contents

(Pregame Warmup)

---Preface---

I awoke in the middle of the night from a dream that took me back to my younger days working at our family's restaurant. I found myself unable to fall back asleep. A flood of thoughts and memories kept rushing through my mind. I could not stop thinking or reliving one memory after another. My sleeplessness dragged on until I finally wore myself out into a deep sleep.

The next afternoon, I told my wife about this experience. We discussed the idea of me writing down this flood of information. There were moments when I considered authoring a book about this special time in my life. Over the next couple of days, I concluded this was no time to start working on another book. If anything, I should return to my futuristic novel, which I have been struggling to finish these past number of years.

Then, about a month or so later, it happened again. I dreamed of the days at my parents' restaurant and awoke only to receive more memories that kept me up for a good part of the night. This recurrence made one thing clear to me. Writing down all these memories might be the only solution if I wanted these sleepless nights to stop.

The original purpose of this book was to give a brief history of my family for our children, grandchildren, and generations to follow. I expected to offer a bit of insight into our generation. It was also evidence of how our faith, strength, and deep-rooted love within our family motivated us all to live a good, clean, proper, prosperous life and to pass it on. I have attempted to categorize these memories into chronological order. They center around the 1960s decade. During this period, my father and mother purchased a popular neighborhood restaurant between Midtown and North St. Louis. I chose this period because of its impact on my growth and psyche. As I began writing, the significance of this period became ever more evident to me.

The 1960s became a very impactful decade in our family. The restaurant my parents purchased was located inside a neighborhood where the white community began fleeing due to the integration of the Black community into this segregated neighborhood. This would contribute to the stressful and challenging economic problems our family business faced. At the same time, my older siblings were growing to their full maturity. This would bring about significant and notable events, changing the look and structure of our family.

As for myself, I grew from childhood to adolescence to young adulthood. The memories captured in this book were the most significant and impactful moments in my young life. I started asking myself why so many of my memories dealt with regret, disappointment, embarrassment, and sorrow. What about all the joyful and wonderful memories encountered during this period? Were those times not as significant or important to me? I have theorized and developed an explanation and understanding as to why these memories are. This is only my subjective belief, and readers are free to choose their explanation or understanding. I anticipate and hope they will consider and examine the cause and creation of their own important and significant life memories.

All those years growing up around my family, the bonds we shared, and the years with my father in our family restaurant created "an unforgettable pastime." Finally, I attempted to consider how all these events have affected the way I feel about things and the other people connected to the outcome of these events in my life. I came to a startling revelation, yet I believe it to be a reasonable conclusion. I have made every attempt to author these stories and events with truth and honesty. You may find a portion of them to be far-fetched and hard to believe. All I can say is nothing is stranger than real life, and this, my reader, was real life.

(The 1st Inning)

---Prior to 1962---

In 1961, my father was financially supporting a family of thirteen. A wife, mother-in-law, and ten children: five boys and five girls. We were one big, Italian-American, and very catholic family. Dad held one full-time and three part-time jobs, working up to sixteen hours a day to make ends meet.

His first part-time job was delivering medicine for a pharmacy owned by one of his cousins. His second part-time job came by way of another cousin, Dr. Pete. A dentist who owned a small building of offices with a parking lot around five blocks from Busch Stadium, home of the St. Louis Cardinals baseball team. My dad and his dentist cousin made the following arrangement.

Whenever the Cardinals were in town playing a ball game at Busch Stadium, Dad and my older brothers would shout out and wave a white towel at passing cars. This was to solicit people to park their cars in our lot if they were going to the ballgame. The proceeds from this venture were split 50-50 between Dad and his cousin, Dr. Pete.

This job of his was my personal favorite because he sometimes allowed me to come along. I would observe my brothers vigorously attempt to flag cars into the lot, yelling out, "Park, Park it right here, Park." I watched as they slowly began filling up the lot, one car at a time. Whenever it got busy with cars pulling into the lot, Dad would let me get out there and continue flagging cars to come in.

Since I was a shy young boy, my attempt to flag cars into the lot was meek and humble. Dad would come over and start shouting at me. At the same time, he would explain to me the proper way for getting cars to pull into the lot. "You need to bark out the words "Park, park it right here, park," he instructed. "And you've got to wave and snap that towel quickly," he added.

Whenever the Cardinals were playing good baseball or a good team came into town, the lot would nearly fill up. However, if they were playing poorly or there was a bad team in town, we would be lucky if the lot filled up halfway. He could usually get anywhere from fifteen to thirty cars in the lot for one dollar a piece.

The best paydays came when the Cardinals were playing a doubleheader. In addition to parking cars along each side of the two buildings, Dad would squeeze another sixteen cars bumper-to-bumper in the middle of the lot between the two sides. Besides that, he would charge a dollar fifty for each car because it was for two games.

There was no time for him to go home for dinner after getting off his day job. So, during the night games, once all the cars parked into the lot and the game started, Mom would stop by and deliver dinner. Sometimes, we sat inside cars in the parking lot and turned on the radio. It was a real privilege hearing the ball games called by Harry Carey and Jack Buck, two of the greatest broadcasters of all time.

I loved Harry Cary because he was so colorful and enthusiastic. I never got tired of hearing him yelling over the radio, "It might be… It could be…It is…a home run." I would sit there and stare up at the stars in the sky and watch as the bats flew around the clock tower across the street at Northside Bank. I considered Jack Buck to be dry and boring until I got a bit older and started listening more closely. His style of wit, humor, and the stories that went along with his play-by-play of the game were pure and rare entertainment.

My Grandma Catherine owned a four-family apartment building in another section of North St. Louis. This was Dad's third part-time job. Grandma began to live with us around the same time I was born. She helped our family out financially through the rent money we collected from the apartment building.

The neighborhood where this apartment was located had already begun seeing the integration of Black residents into the area. On Saturdays, I would go along with Dad and knock on the doors of tenants' homes, attempting to collect the monthly rent. It was always uncertain as to whether we would collect any rent. Every knock on the door would bring various results. For one, tenants would answer the door and pay their rent. Other tenants might ask for more time to produce the rent money, and sometimes, there would be no answer whether they were home or not.

Although it could be a bit of a struggle at times to collect, tenants were paying their rent overall. Other times, I would tag along whenever Dad needed to fix one of the tenant's maintenance issues. There were other times when one of the apartments became vacant. He would then go in and take care of any necessary repairs to get the place all fixed up and ready for new tenants to move in.

Dad was very handy with building maintenance and repairs, a skill he learned from his father. He attempted to pass these skills on to me but with little success. I do not believe that he ever had patience or tolerance for slow learners. Therefore, his aggressive style of teaching proved to be very ineffective for me.

For almost twenty years, his main full-time job was that of a delivery route truck driver for the Hostess Cake Company. Their main products were Twinkies, Cupcakes, and Snowballs. During the Christmas holidays, fruitcakes also became part of their product line. When Dad was first hired by Hostess Cake, there was this policy of no facial hair allowed. The man in charge took one look at Dad's mustache and said, "I like it. It looks good on you; keep it," and instructed him not to shave it off.

Every morning, Dad would go non-stop at breakneck speed to complete an enormous number of cake route stops. He would go in and pull off the old product from the shelves and replace it with a new product before heading off to his next stop. Since he was working day and night to make ends meet, there would be times when he would find it necessary to pull the truck over and rest. This break would be just long enough for him to grab a ten-minute nap, and then he returned to work the route feeling like a new man.

I could offer witnesses attesting that my dad was one of the quickest, fastest, and hardest workers you will ever meet. However, the Belleville, Illinois, route became too big for any one person to manage. During his last few years on the cake route, he would continuously request his supervisor to cut back on the size of the route. Instead, the top boss just kept admonishing him. "Vitale, you are taking way too long to complete that route of yours." he barked. It finally reached a point where the stress of this job was beginning to severely affect his health.

He was nearing fifty years old, and the Hostess Cake truck route was no longer manageable for him to complete every day. Dad would arrive exceedingly early in the morning at the truck depot on Hebert Street. From there, he would begin the long trek of his cake route into Belleville, Illinois. Coincidentally, this depot just happened to be located two blocks from a quaint little neighborhood barbecue restaurant. This little spot would forever leave an indelible impression on me.

The restaurant sat on the corner of Elliott and Sullivan, where this delightful little structure fashioned in brick and stone exuded with charm. This gem of a building was located inside a tranquil neighborhood, gracefully poised between Midtown and North St. Louis, Missouri. From the start of its brief twenty-plus year existence, from the 1950s through the 1960s, it became known for its barbecue ribs. I feel confident in stating that St. Louis is widely known for its barbecue and ribs. The original owner and builder of this little spot was Phil Polizzi, and he aptly called his place Phil's Bar-B-Que.

Phil got his first taste of barbecue at Big John's, another neighborhood joint. "I used to go to Big John's and see how they cooked the ribs," remembered Phil. "I watch, and I watch, and I figure I can do just as good."

So, Phil built a large fire pit behind his house, set up picnic tables in his backyard, and began selling ribs during the summer. "The yard was loaded with people," he recalled, and even Big John came over. He ate my ribs and said, "You dago, you got me beat."

By 1951, Polizzi had erected a more formal rib shack on the corner of Elliot and Sullivan, next door to his house, and had taken on his wife's brother Joe as a partner. The restaurant became so successful that he was able to quit his job as a presser for the Rosenberg Garment Company.

Advertisement from May 11, 1951, St. Louis Post-Dispatch

This little neighborhood spot had gotten quite popular and flourished throughout the 1950s, and as mentioned in the above newspaper clipping, it was located only three blocks east of Sportsman's Park. For anyone unfamiliar with Sportsman's Park, it was home to the St. Louis Browns baseball team (1902-1953) and the St. Louis Cardinals baseball team (mid-1920–1966). In 1953, the park's name changed to Busch Stadium, reflecting the name of the team's new ownership.

As the 1950s ended and a new decade began, people with foresight were witnessing and understanding the beginnings of a slow deterioration of property value in this area of town. It was evident that in the surrounding neighborhoods, people were moving out of the city and migrating as far out as the North and South St. Louis County lines. A steady flow of vacancies from these homes and apartments enabled lower-income people to move into the area. In the 1950s, this area of town was still very segregated, but this recent turn of events was creating fear and uncertainty. These changes were creating a potential risk of lowering neighborhood property values.

When lower-income Black residents moved into certain neighborhoods, white residents tended to move farther out. Throughout the past century, St. Louis had experienced "white flight" - white people progressively moving away from the city's urban center and into the suburbs. Between 1950 and 1970, close to sixty percent of the white population fled the city. After 1970, depopulation of the city, especially the northside area, fell by almost 170,000 based on the 1980 census.

I must admit my family was part of this massive flight from the city. It was 1957, and we were living in a different section of the North St. Louis area. My parents had decided to sell their home in the city and build a new one in North St. Louis County. In our city neighborhood, other neighbors had made attempts to enforce or pressure others not to sell their homes to a Black person. Dad would have none of that, allowing anyone interested to view our home for sale.

Even at the age of five years old, I can distinctly remember the Black couple who came through our home and purchased it. I do not understand why this moment in time was so memorable to me. It may have been the possibility or fact that it may well have been my very first close encounter with a Black person.

In 1958, after moving into our new home, my mother found herself pregnant with the last of her ten children. Our new home came equipped with four bedrooms. Mom and Dad were in one bedroom, and our grandmother, Catherine Deluca, was in another bedroom. This meant only two bedrooms remained for all of us children. My oldest two sisters took one bedroom, and my next two sisters got the other bedroom. My youngest sister slept with our Grandma Catherine in a twin bed. After she got too big to fit in the bed with grandma, my parents squeezed her between my two younger sisters in a double bed.

The question remained: where to put all of us brothers? Well, behind our two-car garage, there just so happened to be this large indoor patio. There were two double beds placed inside this room. My two oldest brothers, Don and Mariano, slept in one of the double beds. My other older brother, Nick, and I slept in the other bed.

There was one other modest problem. The main wall of our room facing the backyard consisted of jalousie windows. These louvered glass panels were in storm doors, enclosed porches, or breezeways and were a common feature of mid-century homes, especially in warmer climates. Typically, these windows enclosed outdoor areas like porches. Thankfully, our mom eventually put curtains or drapes on the glass panels, allowing us more privacy.

During wintertime, our room got very cold, even with the extra heater our dad had placed in the room. My two oldest brothers would always complain about the cold temperatures inside our room. "One day, Mom, you are going to come into our room and find the four of us dead, either from a fire caused by that indoor heater or just from freezing to death," they predicted. Our youngest brother was yet to be born. He would live in the baby crib in our parents' room and, later, slept in a small bed alongside them.

***

Once the 1960s decade arrived, Phil Polizzi was asking himself, should I continue to stay in this neighborhood, or should I consider selling my golden goose and moving to brighter pastures? By late 1961, he finally realized the time had come to sell. For all we know, Phil may have already begun seeing a decline in his business. He set out with a plan to make an offer on the sale of his popular little barbecue restaurant. I can confidently state one person whom he considered to be a potential buyer: my dad. Let me explain how an offer from Phil Polizzi would even be coming my dad's way, and the answer was my mother.

Mariano and Catherine Deluca were an immigrant couple from Italy. They came to the United States after getting married around the turn of the century. This couple, unfortunately, were unable to produce children of their own. Catherine was over forty years old and desperately wanted children in her life. Mariano went looking into the underground market to find and adopt a baby.

Their first adoption was a boy they named Gioacchino, and the second adoption was a girl they named Lena. This was my mother. For a large part of her life, she was frustrated by never knowing who and where she had originally come from. She expressed to me repeatedly this awful feeling of emptiness. For Lena, having ten children was to be her way of filling this void in her life.

My parents made innumerous attempts and went to great lengths and effort trying to discover more details about Mom's roots but with little success. At one point, both were certain they had found the original place where her birth mother had delivered Lena. However, they informed my parents that their birth records were gone due to a previous fire. The only discovery they made was the young mother's name, Elizabeth Rivers.

Through further investigation, there is a distinct possibility that the father of this baby might well have been Mariano Deluca's brother. This is just one more scenario as to how this baby found its way to Mariano and Catherine Deluca. To my way of thinking, my mother's birth and wherever she came from will remain a mystery for all time.

The Deluca's and Polizzi's had a family relationship. Rose Polizzi and my grandmother Catherine Deluca were sisters. Therefore, you might think Phil Polizzi was related to my mother. However, Phil belonged to a different Polizzi family, and there was no relationship between them and the Deluca's. However, it so happened that Phil's wife, Theresa Bono, did have a family relationship with the Deluca's. In fact, Phil and Theresa were both at my parents' bridal wedding party.

Phil Polizzi came to my dad with the following offer. "Vince, I am willing to sell you my restaurant and business," he said. "Besides that, I will stay on and train you with everything you need to know about running this business." he offered. However, there was one thing that could not come from training. That would be Phil's personality, along with his warm, friendly demeanor and charm. Undoubtedly, this served Phil well in cultivating and growing his loyal client base, which repeatedly kept coming back to his restaurant.

Phil sweetened things even further by offering up this deal. "I am going to personally offer you the financing to purchase my business." Of course, this was the only viable way the purchase could have taken place. Dad could not provide any up-front money. Supporting a large family of thirteen on a blue-collar worker's salary made it a certainty that he could not secure a sizable business loan. The asking purchase price was $35,000, and payments would be monthly for ten years at a reasonable fixed interest rate.

However, it would be necessary for Dad to quit three of his jobs to take over a business that he knew nothing about. The income potential was there, but he would need to make this transition successfully and keep the business running at or near its current profitable level. There was another pivotal factor in this decision process. In less than nine months, he was to become eligible for a twenty-year pension from Hostess Cake. If he were to resign, it would mean a total loss of that pension. With that said, he was still considering going forward with Phil's offer. This will attest to how incredibly difficult and unbearable it must have been to continue doing that Hostess Cake route every day. I cannot imagine the painstaking decision process he must have gone through before making a final decision.

My oldest brother, Don, was very skeptical of Phil's offer. "Dad, this man is asking way too much for his place. Before looking into this any further, negotiate with Phil and force him to lower the asking price," he advised. There may have been true relevance in this statement. For example, at this point in history, the McDonald's restaurant chain had over 250 properties throughout the country, and their current franchise price was approximately $12,000.

Phil Polizzi was requesting an extremely high premium price that was based on the restaurant's current popularity and sales. There was no consideration or discussion given to changes in the demographics coming forth in the surrounding neighborhoods. This should have brought into question the viability and strength of the restaurant's future economic outlook. I can almost say with certainty that Dad was completely unaware of taking into consideration these types of sophisticated business studies.

In the meantime, the offer to purchase this restaurant was on the table now, and if he turned it down, Phil would be moving on to look for another potential buyer. After long and thoughtful consideration and deliberation, Dad had made his decision. He would reach out for the proverbial brass ring while at the same time agreeing to pay Phil's inflated asking price.

He turned in his resignation to Hostess Cake within a matter of days, and there would be no turning back. Over the next couple of years, there would be a lengthy list of drivers who took a shot to adequately perform and complete the daily Bellville, Illinois route, but with no success. Management finally came to the realization one person could not complete this route. It left them with no choice but to split the route between two drivers and then, later, a third driver.

When I first discovered we had purchased a restaurant, I was shocked yet happy. How cool was that? My family was the owner of a restaurant. Of course, being only nine years old, I had no idea about the time, effort, or amount of work involved in running this kind of business.

The first few months were uneventful from my point of view. Mom and Dad were going through their restaurant training period. During this time, I was unable to find any opportunity to check out or, for that matter, get a glimpse of the place. After a lengthy bit of time, the training period ended. It was now up to my parents to hold onto and continue the success of this wonderful little brick-and-stone building on Elliott and Sullivan.

Months after selling off his popular barbecue restaurant at Elliott and Sullivan, Phil Polizzi purchased another long-standing barbecue establishment. He had now relocated from North St. Louis to Afton, Missouri. Less than fifteen miles away. This new spot was in a stable middle-class area of town, and in all probability, the reason behind selling off his other place and moving to Afton, Mo.

Jack Polizzi, Phil's cousin, initially became his partner in this new location, and they simply called it Jack's & Phil's. Sometime after 1967, the two parted ways. Incidentally, one of their waitresses had a son who went on to star in movies and television. After he became famous, this woman retired from her position. Her son is the former St. Louisan actor John Goodman.

Phil's new place was initially the size of a living room, and people would line up outside to get a table. By the mid-1970s, the restaurant had expanded to 160 seats, but it was not unusual to still be waiting for a table on weekends. Phil's Bar-B-Que and his successful business lived on.

However, our story is about that little place on the corner of Elliot and Sullivan and the Vitale family who kept it going through the 1960s, along with a cast of supporting characters. The events described herein come from my memories of that period. Admittedly, I was an impressionable young boy growing up from the ages of nine to seventeen in this Black and white neighborhood. Undeniable prejudice and segregation occurred quite frequently throughout the 1960s. It is important to understand my portrayal of the events that took place is strictly based on my perception and what I observed to be happening.

***

In 1938, the first child and eldest son born into the Vitale family was Damiano, named after our paternal grandfather. My brother chose to go by his preferred name, Don. It is an old Italian tradition to name your first son and daughter after your paternal grandfather and grandmother. My parents did not waver from this tradition.

My paternal grandfather Damiano Vitale was a tyrant and, from my understanding, abusive to his wife and children. While still a young man, before the turn of the 20th century, he worked for law enforcement in Northern Italy. During this time, he married his first wife. While giving childbirth, neither his wife nor child survived. Undoubtedly, this must have been a devastating blow to bear, and it pushed him to return to his home in Sicily.

While back in his hometown, another young girl named Patrina Biando captured his interest. Damiano went to her father and asked for her hand in marriage. Patrina was only fifteen years old and nine years younger than Damiano. She showed no interest in wanting to marry this man; besides that, he was already beginning to go bald. Her father gave him a resounding "No," but Damiano was unwilling to take that answer and devised a plan.

He managed to figure out a way to coerce this young girl into a building and then stayed with her overnight by keeping her locked up until the next morning. Rape marriage law was the term for this phenomenon in the 2010s. However, the practice has existed within the legal systems in history and continues to exist in societies today in various forms. Such laws were common around the world until the 1970s.

These women feared being vocal about their assault. They felt guilty for shaming their families and experienced sexual shame and self-blame. It even caused them to develop negative views of themselves as women. Patrina ended up living the rest of her life with a man she never loved. It was an unhappy marriage and a difficult family life for which their children paid the highest price. Although she gave birth to twelve children, Patrina was a bitter woman, and she struggled to care for them. My dad loved his mother. "She tolerated me," he remarked whenever talking about his mother.

After Damiano and Patrina immigrated to the United States around the 1900s, he found work at Laclede Gas Company in St. Louis. Eventually, he would quit his regular job and open a small grocery store. He then began running a bootleg liquor business with a backroom bar, and this happened during the Prohibition (1920-1933) era. Damiano would send his oldest and youngest sons off to learn the trade of cutting hair at barber school. Dad was the middle son and had shown his father signs of real intelligence. At the age of nine years old, he started working by his father's side.

At ten years old, he was managing the grocery store and assisting his father with running the bar and bootleg liquor business. During these years spent in his father's business, he came across shady and unsavory characters and got engaged in tough dealings, fights, and other circumstances that ranged anywhere from bad to evil. This kind of lifestyle caused him to become hardened, a bit wild, and difficult to manage.

Dad never completed the eighth grade. He found no interest or need to attend school. Besides that, his father was dependent upon him working in the business. Although prohibition had ended, Damiano continued to run his liquor business illegally. At first, he paid off the police, but after years of doing this, he grew tired and decided to stop paying.

By the age of twenty-four, Dad had grown into a person unmanageable even for his father. Damiano thought there was only one way to solve and correct this behavior. He would take his son around town, find a nice girl to marry, and hopefully settle him down.

My father was a good-looking man but small in stature at barely five feet four inches tall and weighing under 130 lbs. However, you would be sadly mistaken if you thought or believed you could take this man down easily. Tough and fearless, he was always prepared and ready to do whatever was necessary to defend himself. In working all those years behind his father's bar, Dad became quite experienced at handling himself and others whenever things got rough. At times, his actions could get a little crazy, making him a bit unpredictable.

Grandpa Damiano took Dad to visit a considerable number of young Italian women. The purpose of these visits was to discuss the possibility of an arranged marriage if both families agreed. They had no luck in finding a match. Then, one day, his cousin Louie came by to visit, "Vince, I went to the home of this widow who has this beautiful seventeen-year-old daughter," he explained. "I courted her, but she refused my proposal. I think you should try and visit this girl," advised Louie.

Years later, we discovered from Mom that our cousin Louie, for whatever reason, did not appeal to her in any way. My Grandma Deluca told my mother, "I think you should marry this man." At that point, Lena became overly dramatic and stated firmly but plainly, "If you make me marry him, I will kill myself."

This opened the door for my grandfather to arrange a meeting with the Deluca's. Vince and Lena were immediately attracted to each other and quickly nodded in agreement to liking what they saw in each other. After a formal courtship, they were married in 1937 and became one. Lena was not only beautiful, but she was also tall and slender, reaching a height of around five feet seven inches. It may have had something to do with his own small stature, but Dad always had this great attraction and affection for things big, large, or tall.

Grandpa Damiano was right. His son finding a good woman and getting married eventually did settle him down to become a faithful and loyal husband and father. Unfortunately, it took time to calm down his intense and unruly nature and demeanor. My oldest brother, Don, had become one of the recipients of this unruly behavior. One day, Dad came home from work and suddenly noticed this look of fear and terror showing on his son's young face. Understanding that he could be the only person responsible for this, Dad vowed right there and then to subdue his unorthodox ways and behavior.

Not once, but twice, Dad took his father's place and served a jail sentence for the illegal sale of alcohol. The first time, my oldest brother was only two weeks old, and the second time, my second brother was only six months old. After that, he realized it was time to quit his father's business and find work elsewhere for the welfare of his family.

***

After graduating from high school, Don made the decision to continue furthering his education. Dad made it clear that there was no money for him to attend any college or university. The idea of higher education for his son never crossed our father's mind. That was more for the affluent families who could afford to meet these kinds of financial demands.

Don was not going to allow this obstacle to get in the way of achieving a higher-level educational goal. However, he still needed acceptance into a college or university. Mom took the initiative and spoke with her cousin, Phyllis, one of the older children in her Aunt Rose's family. The success in their pecan business had afforded them tight connections with St. Louis University, and she secured a meeting for my mom and brother to speak with the administrator.

Saint Louis University is a private Jesuit research university founded in 1818 by Louis William Valentine DuBourg. It is the oldest university west of the Mississippi River and the second-oldest Jesuit university in the United States. After meeting with the administrator, Don managed to secure an acceptance letter into the university.

When my parents first took over the restaurant business, my oldest brother, Don, had already graduated from St. Louis University. He landed a position at Mercantile Bank and Trust and was doing everything possible to make the most out of this opportunity.

Even before starting to help at the restaurant on Fridays, Don had worked at the parking lot flagging cars down for St. Louis Cardinals baseball home games. His biggest concern and fear was if someone from the bank spotted him. Don had worked extremely hard to get to this point in his life. He could not risk embarrassment or have anything else happen that might spoil the current opportunity with Mercantile Bank and Trust. Fortunately, all his fears were unfounded, and he would later go on to achieve professional and financial success.

***

In 1940, the second child born into the family was Mariano, named after our maternal grandfather. Grandpa

Mariano was a prosperous man who, over the years, had acquired properties. Back in those days, the area where he lived was under the influence of the mafia, who required payment for protection. One time, this henchman came over to collect, but Mariano refused to pay, and instead, he picked up an axe and killed the man. His mistake was not disposing of the body properly. The mafia put the missing pieces together and discovered what happened.

Lena was only seven years old when she witnessed her father murdered by gunshot in the footsteps of their home. Over the next ten years, she lived with her mother, who became obsessively protective and fearfully paranoid about their safety. Lena was an intelligent young girl, but she contracted Scarlet Fever at an early age, which then developed into Rheumatic Fever. After her bout with this illness, she later confessed to me that her mind was never quite the same. A combination of developing this sickness along with her mother's constant fearmongering drove her to finally stop attending school at the seventh-grade level.

Grandma Deluca was inexperienced and ignorant in the handling of finances. Over time, this resulted in their sizable wealth diminishing. By the time Lena reached seventeen years of age, her mother came to the realization it was time to consider finding a suitor for her daughter. That is how my cousin Louie and dad got the opportunity to meet with her. Grandma was hoping the right person might come along to lighten or improve their financial situation.

In my family, for whatever reason, the boys might turn out to be late bloomers, reaching their full potential later in life than expected. This was quite likely the situation with my brother Mariano, and it caused him to struggle through his early educational process. After graduating from Catholic grade school, Don, and then later Mariano, enrolled in seminary school. It was our mother's wish and desire that they might someday enter the priesthood. However, after spending enough time in the seminary, Don realized that he liked girls too much and had to walk away from this vocation.

On the other hand, Mariano happened to believe this very well might be his calling. Unfortunately, it was a great struggle for him to pass their academic classes. The seminary had no choice but to release him. It is difficult to understand the expulsion of a person wanting to dedicate their life to God because they did not meet a certain level of academic excellence. This was my brother's fate.

Mariano always gave of himself in helping with our family's needs. After graduating from high school, it was apparent his educational prowess was not particularly strong. Our father still had no financial means to permit another son to consider going off to college. Besides that, he needed his son's help and support to fulfill the needs of our large family of thirteen. Dad would do what he thought was best and send him off to work. Mariano accepted employment with Hostess Cake as one of their bakers.

***

In 1942, the third child and eldest daughter born into the family was Patricia, named after my paternal grandmother. When she began having difficulty achieving acceptable grades during her sophomore year of high school, Dad said to her. "Patricia, I think it is time that you consider looking into a trade school for your future education." He mentioned the possibility of attending a beauty school and becoming a hairstylist. "Yes, that type of work does sound appealing to me," she responded.

Patricia attended a beautician school for six months and immediately began working at a beauty parlor. At that point, her only other ambition was finding the right man that would lead to marriage.

And then it happened…one evening before dinner, Patricia announced to her sisters, "Something good is going to happen to me tonight." This evening, she was going to meet someone special. She spoke with her younger sister, Catherine. "I know Rosemary isn't too happy with us right now, but I need you to call and convince her to pick us up so we can all go out together," she explained. You see, their girlfriend had a car, and my sisters needed a ride.

Patricia had gotten anxious to the point where she was unable to eat dinner that evening. Rosemary came through and picked the girls up. However, the question remained as to where they should go. Since it was Patricia who had this revelation, they decided she was the one who should choose. At first, she said, "I don't care, just go anywhere," but then the answer came to her. "Let's go to the bowling alley," she decided.

While they were bowling, Patricia noticed a handsome young man dressed in a suit talking to bowlers in another lane. She kept thinking of ways to try and meet him but realized it was not going to happen and tried to forget it. Rosemary started making her way over to the snack bar, and this young man, whom Patricia had noticed earlier, was heading in the same direction. Stepping up to the bar, he smiled and greeted her, "Hello, Rosemary."

His name was Steve Letko, a friend of Rosemary's boyfriend, so they knew each other. They started talking, and she suggested that he come over to meet her friends. The girls were continuing to bowl, and then Rosemary returned with a young man in tow. When Patricia turned around and saw him standing there, her heart fluttered. The two of them would spend the rest of the evening together simply talking.

When it came time for them to leave, Steve asked to see her again. Once she arrived back home, Patricia ran over to Mom and announced, "I have met the man that I am going to marry." Her prediction would go on to become history. However, the fact remains that we will never know whether this was a prophetic phenomenon or a self-fulfilling prophecy.

***

In 1943, the fourth child born into the family was Catherine, named after our maternal grandmother. She was only one year younger than Patricia. Dad handed over the same offer he gave his first daughter. "Next year, after Patricia completes beauty school and begins working, I will send you there, too," he stated. Catherine was a good student, and there was no need for her to attend a trade school. The thing is, she has always been the type of person to go with the flow and not make waves. Besides, she was not particularly happy at school and teased by others about the way she dressed. When you do not have the money to wear nice clothes, you must be very inventive in how you dress.

At one point, Catherine suggested an interest in secretarial school, but my father responded, "What for? So, you can sit on a guy's lap?" After this absurd comment, the conversation came to a quick end. Once again, any thoughts or ideas about a college education were not under consideration. Our father was doing what he felt and believed was the best alternative. Catherine followed her sister and attended the beauty school.

The four oldest children were now all working and living at home. Dad could not financially assist his oldest son's university education. So, Don worked part-time evenings and weekends at Kroger's grocery store and full-time in the summer at Continental Can Company to pay for his tuition.

The other three children willingly contributed the greater portion of their income to support the family's growing financial needs. Patricia and Catherine had no mode of transportation to get to work. In the meantime, Mom would have to drive both my sisters to and from their respective beauty shops every day and night.

***

In 1944, the fifth child, my brother Nick, was born into the family. They named him after one of my dad's brothers. While my Mom was pregnant with my brother, they drafted my dad to serve in the Army at the age of 32 years old. This occurred during the latter part of World War II. The army gave him an IQ test, and the score was high enough to get him into the Air Force. They sent him to flight gunner school for training. All the other gunners were mostly between the ages of 18 and 22. Dad fell victim to constant stress and anxiety in being away from his wife and children, who needed him more than the U.S. government.

I recall one story Dad told me while flying during one of his practice missions. The commanding officer started shouting out orders to the men, "Bailout practice." All the young men quickly began strapping on their parachutes. The officer spotted Dad sitting there, not making a move. He advanced toward this stoic body that had yet to budge from its seat, "I said bail-out practice," he shouted once again. Looking up at the commanding officer, Dad simply replied, "There is nothing wrong with this plane. Why do you want me jumping out of it?" The officer snapped back at him, "Who in the hell said anything about jumping out of this plane? I just want to see how fast you can get that parachute on." Instantly, Dad jumped out of his seat and quickly strapped on the parachute, responding, "Oh, I can do that real fast."

During another one of his practice missions, he fell victim to a severe injury. The only thing Dad remembered was sitting in the gunner's hole on the plane and firing away. Suddenly, he felt this strong sensation of pain, as if someone had him on the back of the head with a sledgehammer. He was in the hospital for weeks to come. The war in Europe was now over. Due to his illness and age, along with having a wife and five children, the army mercifully discharged him from service duty.

Don and Mariano were much older than Nick and had shown little interest in spending time with their younger brother. So, he chose to spend his early years hanging out with his two older sisters, Patricia and Catherine. Over time, it became quite evident Nick was turning out to be your typical, good old American boy who loved fast cars and girls. In his young teen years, he found himself in constant trouble when caught making out with one girl after another in our basement.

He got a job working for Giovanni's, an Italian import grocery store. Mom loved going to this store where she did her grocery shopping. I will never forget her saying to me back then, "Your father gives me fifty dollars a week and expects me to buy everything that is needed for the whole family."

Nick's main duty at Giovanni's was to take care of the large produce stand outside the store. When he was not working or spending time with a girl, you might find him tinkering around cars. He turned out to be quite the rebel. According to him, it is nothing short of a miracle that he survived all those things that he had never told us about.

One thing he luckily did survive was running away from home. I say this because he was fortunate our father and mother did not kill him. Thankfully, over the years, our family has managed a good laugh over this whole incident, although it was anything but funny at the time.

We all awoke one morning to find Mom acting hysterically. She stopped wailing long enough to read my brother's runaway note aloud before starting all over again. "My friend, Bill Turner, and I are leaving home to find our way. Please do not worry about me. I am going to be fine." The boy he was running away with was nothing but trouble. This only gave my parents more reason to be concerned.

Coincidentally, it happened to be our brother Don's first day of work in his business career at Mercantile Bank and Trust. It would not be long before he joined in Mom's hysteria after discovering the few business suits that he owned were gone. The suits, which Nick had taken along with him, were gone forever. In the meantime, Don had to fit his way into one of our dad's undersized suits for his first big day on the job.

Nick was only seventeen years old when he ran off, and we had no idea where he went. Little did we know that he and his friend had taken off for California. The next few weeks were excruciatingly painful. It was not so much because Nick ran away, although we were all terribly upset and concerned for him. To me, the bigger problem was having to endure, experience, and witness all the wild emotions and antics of our mother.

During the first week, we younger kids would pile into the car and drive around the entire city looking and searching for our brother. Mom would stick her head out the car window and shout out his name sporadically and repeatedly. After this behavior went on for a while, I started asking myself, what is she doing? We were searching for my brother, not a lost dog.

If nothing else, those few weeks taught me the incredibly deep emotional love Mom has for us children. I have tried to understand things from her point of view. These children were all she had of herself. Adopted while still a baby, she had no idea who or where she came from. She spent her life keeping a tight hold on the love of her children. Throughout these years, she would experience anxiety, stress, and much needless worry over her children, as one by one, she watched them go through all the normal expeditions and struggles of life.

For now, all that mattered was that one of her children had gone missing. In her heart and mind, Mom appeared unable to tolerate or cope with the possibility of her son never returning. I was becoming concerned that if he did not come back home, she might not survive. By the grace of God, the day came when Nick found himself completely out of money with nowhere to turn, and he wired us to get bus fare home.

If he could have held out for a little longer, Nick believes there was a job opportunity that was going to come his way. If that had occurred, there is no telling if or when we might have seen our brother again. Ironically, he returned on Thanksgiving Day, giving us that much more to be thankful for because our brother and son had come back home.

Dad was extremely upset with Nick for running off and putting our family through all this pain. His wrath was about to come down hard on my brother. However, for the good of our family and to appease my mother's wishes, he miraculously kept his emotions under control and put this unfortunate piece of history in the past.

***

In 1946, the sixth child born into the family was Theresa, named after one of mom's favorite saints. Ste. Thérèse Lisieux became canonized in 1925 when mom was still a little girl. Thérèse has been a highly influential model of sanctity for Catholics and others because of the simplicity and practicality of her approach to spiritual life. Together with Saint Francis of Assisi, she is one of the most popular saints in the history of the church. Mom owned and kept loving care over two exceptionally large statues of these saints within our home.

As a young girl, Theresa kept to herself and was one of the quiet ones in our family. In her later high school years, she broke out of her shell. There came along this one very tall, skinny young man with glasses named Ron, whom she dated for a couple of years. They had this strange relationship that I never understood. One minute, they were kissing, and the next minute, they could be arguing and fighting. Sometimes, these arguments would get animated and loud. These events occurred off and on for a long portion of their time together.

One evening, the whole thing finally came to a climax. Ron was hanging around outside our house and would not leave. Mariano came out and informed him. "It's time for you to go." Ron did not see things that way, so my brother tried persuading him with a fist in his face.

Mom received a phone call about this altercation at our house. She made her way back home and found Ron standing on our front lawn. Getting out of her car, the young man went running over, holding a blood-stained handkerchief around his nose. His final words as he walked by were, "Look at what your son did to me." That was the last time we saw him, and from my family's point of view, it was a great relief.

***

In 1949, Lucia, the seventh child born in our family, was named after St Lucia, the patron saint of the blind. From an early age, Lucia would be the first out of bed in the morning. She had this desire and need to go throughout the house, letting everyone know that it was time to get up.

Her given name is related to an incident that happened to one of my older sisters. When Catherine was a young child, she got hold of a pencil and proceeded to stick it into her eye. At the Doctor's office, they informed my mother the damage done by the pencil would leave her daughter permanently blind in that eye. Unwilling to accept this prognosis, Mom began to pray.

She went to church and prayed even more for Catherine to somehow retain her eyesight. She prayed to God and reached out to St Lucia, the patron saint of the blind. One day, while praying at the church, she heard a voice saying to her, "What are you doing here? Go home," and she took this to mean everything was going to be all right.

On their next visit to the doctor's office, Mom received news that the specific problem related to Catherine's eye was suddenly gone. She became overjoyed and incredibly grateful to know her daughter's eyesight issue had disappeared. Whether it was a miracle or not, mom made a promise that if she ever gave birth to another girl, she would name her after St. Lucia.

***

As for myself, I was the eighth child born into the family. My birth occurred on the day that General Dwight David Eisenhower won his first presidential election, November 4, 1952. Induction of childbirth by doctors was not a customary practice in those days. According to my mother, it would be a total of ten months before I willingly made my grand entrance into the world. I guess that should have been a clue and a warning to me. I was going to be one of those males in my family who are slow to mature.

In coming out of the womb, my size took everyone by surprise: a long baby weighing in at around eleven pounds. My father, being impressed with bigger things, was quite ecstatic over the size of his new son. The doctor took one look at me and proclaimed, "You've got a football player here." And later, the doctor informed my mother that I was also double-jointed.

In addition to its being the presidential election, there was one other incredibly special thing that happened around my birth. During her stay in the hospital, my mother discovered the archbishop of St. Louis was there visiting. She managed to corral him and requested a blessing for me. I have always believed this to be something extra special that she went out of her way to do for me.

The day that I came home, my other siblings were anxiously awaiting my arrival. They took one look at me and, with great disappointment in their voice, announced, "That's not a baby."

***

In 1954, the ninth child born into the family was my sister, Maria, which is the Italian name for Mary. Mom felt a very faithful and special connection with Mary, the blessed mother of Jesus Christ. The fact that Mom was pregnant again, five months after my birth, tells me this pregnancy was quite unexpected.

Maria was born and weighed exactly five pounds, barely avoiding a stay in the hospital incubator at birth. My family would tease me that after Mom had a massive baby like me, she did not have anything left in the tank to give our sister, Maria. This comment is related to her small physical size at birth. However, it certainly was not true in any other way, shape, or form. She was a very feisty young girl and strongly opinionated. We had our fair share of arguments and fights because she was not afraid to speak her mind. The nasty comments and remarks directed at me did not sit well, and I would retaliate with my own very harsh remarks toward her. We both regretted those days, but it seemed unavoidable once our two sharply contrasting ways and personalities collided.

***

In 1958, the tenth and last child born into the family was my brother, Rio. After my parents' investigation into the checking of my mother's background, they were convinced her biological mother's name was Elizabeth Rivers. The name of a river in Italian is Rio, and this has been my understanding of their reasoning for choosing that name.

Rio was born with fair skin and very curly, flaming red hair. As the baby of the family, Rio could easily draw attention to himself, and he loved it. At Christmas time, when he was barely one year old, our family purchased this eight-millimeter movie camera, and Rio became the star of the film. Wearing a cute little blue jumpsuit, he ran around in a small circle and flapped his arms up and down as if he were attempting to fly. The younger children would gather around and encourage him to strut his stuff. I must say that we were guilty of spoiling him during his childhood. And if you ever tried to leave him out of anything he wanted to be a part of, look out.

In my being his older brother directly in front of him, Rio might have looked up to me while we were younger. Later in life, it turned out to be the other way around. Rio himself may well have been a bit of a late bloomer himself, like Mariano and me. Getting married quite likely helped in getting him over that hump. From there, his success and achievements have continued to grow.

(The 2nd Inning)

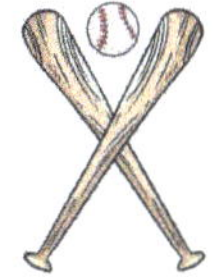

---1962---

The needs of our large family were becoming greater with each passing year. One way to meet these demands was to bring in more income than Dad was earning from all his jobs. This provided even more reasons and purpose for why my parents had chosen this path of restaurant ownership. The hope and expectation were to make enough money off the restaurant business to meet the needs of our family.

With the business under new ownership, all the moves and decisions going forward rested on the shoulders of the man running things, my dad. His first order of business was the staff, which is the bloodstream of any business. During the training period, he was pleased with the performance of all the current employees and saw no reason to make changes.

Laverne was our daytime waitress; Bee was our nighttime waitress. A third waitress, Sonja, helped part-time. Besides taking orders and serving the dining room guests, these women helped with carryout orders and the cash register. Fred and Nancy were the fry cooks. Their main job was to take care of the fryer station and assist in other areas of the kitchen wherever needed. The remaining employees consisted of Mom, Dad, and my older brothers.

The restaurant was open Tuesday through Saturday, and the hours were long. Weekday hours were from 11 a.m. to 1 a.m., and on Fridays and Saturdays, it stayed open till 1:30 a.m. The work schedule was all set. Mom would arrive around 9:30 a.m., and Laverne would arrive shortly thereafter and help get everything ready for the restaurant's opening. Dad showed up around 11:30 a.m., right before the noon rush began, and stayed through closing. Mom would make her way home in the late afternoon and continue doing household chores, preparing dinner for the family, and seeing to the needs of her children and elderly mother.

The night waitress, Bee, came in to relieve Laverne and started her shift around 5 p.m. along with one of the fry cooks, Fred or Nancy. At closing time, the restaurant had to wash down, and all food and kitchen equipment was put away in preparation for the next day. Then, Dad would begin making his long journey from the city to the north county, arriving home just before 3 a.m. This left him with barely enough time to rest up before going at it all over again the next day.

Friday and Saturday were the two busiest days of the week. On these days, the restaurant would require one additional person for the double duty of a dishwasher and pizza maker. My parents' first year in the business turned out to be a lucrative one. The weekly restaurant sales ranged anywhere from $1,000 – $1,600 per week. During the winter months, sales would drop down to almost $1,000 per week. In the summer months, they would rise as high as $1,600 per week. I can still recall my father telling me our restaurant's economic rule of thumb. When sales were around $1000 per week, they were able to meet their obligations. Once sales crossed their threshold of $1,000, the sales over that amount offered a significant profit.

***

When Grandma Deluca first moved in with the family, she was extremely helpful in assisting Mom with caring for all of us children. After we had moved into our north county home, her health slowly began to decline as she went well past the age of eighty years old. She became quite unhappy and upset with her son-in-law for purchasing the restaurant. This created more work for her daughter. It also meant there would be less available time to spend with her.

Instead of being helpful, it was evident that Grandma was becoming more dependent and demanding of our mother's time. At first, she insisted on going with our mother to the restaurant every day. However, within less than a year, she could no longer deal with the everyday journey back and forth while sitting alone with nothing to do inside the restaurant for hours on end.

Occasionally, in the later part of the evening, Mom just wanted to get a little break from it all. She would take my sisters and go for a drive to Steak 'n Shake. On rare occasions, they allowed me to go along for the ride. Back then, it was a small diner, and the big attraction was their popular curbside service. My sisters would order soft drinks and sometimes buy an order of French fries. It was a big treat for the girls to get out and gab, spot a cute boy or two, and mingle with the male curbside waiters. In the meantime, Grandma would sit on the couch in the family room, lamenting over our mother leaving her side.

She spoke in Italian and had no real grasp of the English language. Except for Mom and Dad, everyone else did not understand a great amount of this foreign language. At times, it could be exceedingly difficult to communicate with Grandma, but we still loved her dearly.

Sometimes, I walked by her bedroom, and there was no doubt what she was doing, praying the rosary. Every one of her rosary beads was the size and color of a large black bean. The rosary chain was over three feet long, and only nuns in the church possessed this kind of rosary. A large portrait of her late husband, Mariano, hung high on the wall. He sat there in his chair, staring down at her. At times, she would begin wailing in his direction, "Mariano, come down from there," demanding him to come out of the picture.

Every so often, one of my grandmother's nephews, Father Salvatore, would come over to visit her and my mother. Back in the early days, my grandmother lost both her husband and son. She lived alone with her young daughter Lena, my mother. Grandma agreed to help her sister, Rose, who herself had eleven children. She took little Salvatore under her wing and into her home for a couple of years during the boy's early childhood. During this time, Mom and Salvatore grew a close family bond with each other.

Occasionally, Mom would take Grandma and us younger children to visit my Great Aunt Rose. This was my grandmother's sister. There is a remarkably interesting fairy tale-type story that happened in this family around thirty years earlier.

Rose and her husband, Joe, were in the process of raising their large young family. One day, they came upon an extremely sick bum in dire need of help and medical attention. They took this man into their home, and Rose nursed him back to health. The way my mother tells it, this man had accumulated and lost fortunes during his lifetime. The man wanted to find a way to thank Rose for all her kindness. He persuaded the family to purchase a used pecan shelling machine. The next thing was to work to get this machine up and running again. This was to be their start in the building of a family-owned pecan business.

He instructed them on how to get the business off the ground. After working on his prescribed system, over time, they managed to make enough money to begin operating a pecan processing factory. This business turned out to become an extremely lucrative and profitable business. It continued to grow and flourish over the next couple of decades. The family eventually made enough money to purchase a home in the township of Ladue. At that time, it was the most prestigious area in St. Louis.

For us children, it was fun to visit this rich neighborhood and see inside their big, beautiful home. We spent time with Great Aunt Rose and her four adult children who lived there. Two of the sons were married, and one, Father Salvatore, became a priest. Three of her daughters were married, and another had joined the convent and became a nun. Her other son and three daughters never married, and they lived out their lives inside this small mansion. Although they were Mom's relatives too, she could never overcome the thought of adoption, and it left her with a feeling of emptiness.

***

When my parents first went into the restaurant business, I was living and enjoying life with no cares or worries. I was only nine years old with no involvement in this business venture. Soon, this would change as we moved closer to the end of our first year in the business. My current regret was not being one of the altar boys at my parish school and church, St. Casimir. The problem was my laziness or capability to learn all the Latin prayers required to become an altar boy.

Dad was working non-stop to meet the demands of running a family-owned restaurant business. Mom spent much of her time helping with those demands. The balance of her time would be for keeping up with household responsibilities, which included cooking, cleaning, washing, and shopping, among other duties. This meant there was no time for either of them to get involved with any after-school activities.

I wanted to play baseball, so my parents signed me up to play at my Catholic school. My team practiced once during the week, and then we played one ball game on the weekend. I would walk myself to the baseball field located behind the school for baseball practice at the scheduled time.

This went on for a brief period, then one evening at practice, a baseball caught me square in the mouth. It was very painful, but I was determined to stay through the end. By the time I arrived home, my front tooth on the left side was throbbing and hurting badly. My dinner was sitting on the kitchen table. I was so hungry that I did not even bother to mention the baseball incident or my aching, painful tooth.

Due to the pain in my tooth, I could only bite and chew with one side of my mouth. Starving for my dinner, I bit into a chicken drumstick and did not chew the meat properly. Suddenly, I could not catch my breath. I could not swallow. Standing up and gasping for air, I heard Mom screaming aloud, "Oh my God, he is choking," and she began to reach for the telephone.

My brother, Mariano, came running into the room to find out what the commotion was all about. My mother pointed in my direction, "Your brother is choking," she shouted. Quickly assessing the situation, he picked me up and turned me upside down. Mariano then began shaking me vigorously and banging my head on the floor. Looking down, I spotted a small sliver of a bone and loudly announced, "It's out, it's out."

Thank God it came out because if there was any more shaking and banging, I might have needed surgery for brain damage. I am certain everyone knows of the Heimlich maneuver. My brother's desperate move in dislodging this tiny bone from my throat has become known as the "saltshaker maneuver." Admittedly, he saved my life, and it was not the first time.

When I was less than two years old, the door going into the basement of our home was mistakenly open. I stood looking down from the top of our open staircase. As I continued to stare downward, I found myself suddenly falling and bouncing down the stairs. Mariano was in the basement and, hearing the noise, came running. He caught me on the last bounce. Otherwise, I would have landed hard on a cement floor. The ligaments in my legs were torn, and my poor mother had no choice but to carry around this huge two-year-old boy for weeks to come.

Surprisingly, the infamous "saltshaker maneuver" did not end there. It made a return appearance around twenty-five years later. By this point in time, I was the only child still living at home with my parents. It was just the three of us as we sat down to dinner and prepared to enjoy a good, juicy-looking steak dinner.

Mom had this tendency to cut her steak into generous-sized pieces. She must have been chewing on an exceptionally large piece that she did not properly chew up and began choking.

Jumping from my seat, I sprang into action by attempting to apply the Heimlich maneuver but with no success. I began to panic and fear my time was running out to dislodge the obstruction from her throat.

I switched methods and, with quick thinking, changed to the "saltshaker maneuver." Picking my mother up and turning her upside down, I vigorously began shaking her up and down. It was not a pretty sight, but it worked, and we all felt a huge sigh of relief. Although I felt a bit ridiculous in performing this maneuver, I felt certain it would work. There was no way that I was going to allow my mother to die of choking on my watch.

As far as my ever going back to achieve a future in baseball, it never materialized. After the ball in the mouth and the chicken bone in the throat incident, I lost my desire to play organized ball for the rest of the year. There were no words of encouragement forthcoming or efforts by my parents to actively reengage me in organized baseball. Opportunities to get back into playing baseball never materialized. Any further baseball I played was of my own accord and choosing.

Like in my earlier days, taking trips alongside Dad collecting rent money or going to the parking lot flagging down cars, I started asking if I could go along to the restaurant. All I wanted was to be around my dad. And so it began, with me going there every Saturday and spending the entire day. We would leave home around 11 a.m. and did not arrive back home until early the next morning.

The first time I entered our restaurant, my reaction was a surprise, realizing it was a much bigger place than I imagined. Being young and impressionable, it was a big thrill getting a closer look and inspection of the inner workings of a restaurant.

I walked around the entire place, taking in every bit of it; undoubtedly proud and quite impressed at everything I took in with my eyes and ears. Although I was still too young to help, I wanted to be a part of what was happening there, not to mention that the main reason was to be with my father.

At least from my point of view, this building on Elliot and Sullivan, particularly the setup inside, was somewhat of a masterpiece for its time. A wide city sidewalk stretched out and around the building. The outer building had three sections. The right side had a reddish-brown brick with a flat asphalt roof. The height inside, from floor to ceiling, was no more than eight feet. This section of the building was the main dining room, approximately forty feet long and twenty-five feet wide. There was a grouping of small windows spaced about six feet apart around the room.

The center section of the building was large grayish-white stones with a rugged front surface. This part of the building stood higher than the other two sections. It had the same flat asphalt roof with smokestack pipes coming out the back section of the roof. These pipes released smoke coming from the huge indoor fire pit. The smell of ribs cooking inside this large fire pit filled the air throughout the block. This center section of the building was well over ten feet high.

The restaurant had a wide front entrance with a metal door and a small window that you could peek through to see inside comfortably. On each side of the door were these large picture windows painted with the restaurant's new name, Vitale's Bar-B-Que. This section of the building is where the main door entrance to the restaurant was located. Strangely enough, there was a swinging glass door on the corner of the building that we kept locked, I assume to keep customers from exiting the dining area without paying.

The left outer side of the building consisted of more reddish-brown bricks with two more windows and another flat asphalt roof. This section was for additional dining space with restrooms located at the end of the building. Directly to the right and behind this entire area was additional kitchen space.

At the end of the building, there was a high chain-linked fence extending out away from the building for about ten feet. From that point, a regular size chain link fence extended down along the right side of the building and then around the entire backside. The ground inside the fenced area was concrete and void of any grass. To the left side of the yard was Phil Polizzi's former home; this house was now under the care of his oldest son, Vince Polizzi.

Approaching the restaurant's entrance for the first time, I stared up at this lighted red neon sign hanging high above the front door. It read Phil's Bar-B-Que, but that sign would eventually come down. For now, it stood as a remembrance of where and how it all began.

Opening the door, and just to my right, I spotted a double gumball machine with a slot for one penny. Entering through the door and immediately to my left, a red patterned table with three chairs was set up against the corner of the wall, just under one of the large picture windows. At the end of the short wall to the left of the table, I noticed a payphone. Across from the payphone was a mechanical cigarette machine with twenty or more name brands. After depositing coins, you would locate the cigarette brand of your choice and pull out the round metal knob below that brand. A pack of the cigarettes selected dropped to the bottom of an open tray.

To the left was a small dining cove area. On the right side were two tables, each with one red booth on one side and chairs on the other side. On the left side of the cove was a long red booth going wall-to-wall, and across from it were tables and chairs. Further into the room, another small opening with space big enough to fit a white pedestal sink and an oval mirror above it. To the left of this were two doors marked men's and women's restroom.

Turning my attention away from the front section, I made my way to the right and headed toward the main dining room. To enter the dining room, you must take one step down with a helpful sign hanging from the ceiling above stating, "Watch Your Step." Immediately to the right was a bright and colorful-looking jukebox. Music played out of the speakers with sounds from great musical artists such as Frank Sinatra, Dean Martin, Tony Bennet, Ray Charles, Chuck Berry, Sam Cooke, The Platters, Jerry Lee Lewis, Elvis Presley, Bobby Darin, Buddy Holly, Ricky Nelson, Johnny Cash, Patsy Cline, and Peggy Lee.

One of the records in the jukebox became my favorite instrumental song of all time, 'Green Onions' by Booker T. and the M.G.s. One ironic thing about this band, which I was unaware of, is that it consisted of two Black and two white men. Amid all this "white flight" from the city and the segregated neighborhoods, we find a couple of Black and white musicians working together to make great music.

There was one particularly special thing about this jukebox; my family got to play it for free. As I understood it, the vendor who brought in the jukebox made this deal. We got a split of all the money put into the machine by our customers. In time, after the vendor had collected a specific amount of money, we would become sole owners of this machine. In the meantime, if we wanted to play it free of charge, all we had to do was paint a quarter with a magic marker. This allowed for the selection of five songs; years later, it would only be three songs. When the machine vendor emptied the jukebox of its coins, he would return the marked quarters to us.

To the left of me was another large stainless-steel cooler filled with various kinds of beers. In the dining room area sat a grouping of tables and chairs. All booths, tables, and chairs in the place had a red pattern. On the right side of the room was a long booth stretching the entire length of the wall. Tables and chairs were set down across from the long booth. A good portion of the tables were only big enough for two people. This was so you could easily put tables together side by side to accommodate any number of guests.

Next to the large beer cooler was a higher table used to place food orders for dining room guests. Against the far corner wall, there was a coffee station and, next to that, a soda fountain machine. Then came a large tabletop with trays for coffee cups and drink glasses. Next to that was a small stand displaying Hostess Cake products. I suppose it may have been a bit of sentimentality on Dad's part to allow the sale of his former company's cake products at our restaurant.

At the far end of this long tabletop sat a large fake wooden barrel with only the front half. Sticking out of the front half barrel was a large brown handle with a spout. On the barrel was a small sign that read C-P Root Beer. I loved root beer but never really cared for the taste of this brand. It just did not have that sharp root beer flavor or the right taste.

Years later, I can still recall a quiet time in the evening when business was not going so great for us. Dad and I were sitting at one of the dining room tables. Pointing up toward the fake barrel, I asked, "Hey, Dad, what does the C-P on the root beer barrel stand for?" He did not take but a second to respond, causing me to laugh out loud as I fondly agreed with his response, "City Piss," he sharply commented.

On the left side of the dining room, past the root beer barrel, was the backside of another seating booth with a long table and two chairs on the other side of it. This was the booth where restaurant employees would sometimes sit when it was not too busy. If business were slow, I would sometimes head for this spot, taking a break from the food order counter and kitchen. Past this booth was another long seating booth going down the entire side wall with more tables and chairs across from it. Lastly, up high on the right-end corner of the room hung a nineteen-inch black and white television. Altogether, I would estimate the restaurant could easily hold eighty dine-in customers.

I took a step up, out of the dining room, and back into the entrance area. To my immediate right was this long steam table. Behind the steam table was a humongous, glossy white brick indoor fire pit. The left side of the pit had two black steel doors with two small windows. On the door was a sliding pole for locking it in place. This was the cooking section of the pit where you could fit as much as twenty-five slabs of ribs. The pit went so deep that it required a long pitchfork with a three-foot wooden handle to reach the back row of ribs. On the right side of the pit was a single black steel door; this was the warming area. You only wanted so many ribs soaking in barbecue sauce at one time. This section allowed the ribs to stay warm without getting too soft from soaking in barbecue sauce.

On the outer section of the long steam table were two long glass windows with a long stainless-steel countertop. If tall enough, you could lay your arms on top of the stainless-steel top. At the same time, you could bend over and peer through the glass to gaze upon the meats and sauces kept warm inside the steam table. The steam table held these large round containers. Four of the containers held slabs of ribs soaking in barbecue sauce. There were two other large containers, one filled with chili and the other with spaghetti sauce and meatballs. Then came two more oblong containers, one holding roast beef and the other roast pork, the meat just sitting there soaking in their gravy juices.

Attached and stretching alongside the back of the steam table was a foot-wide wooden prep table used to prepare food orders. The dining plates sat on a metal shelf under the prep table area. The paper plates for to-go orders sat on the steel countertop above the steam table. Also, underneath the steam table were two large rolls of white paper, one roll wider than the other. These were for wrapping up the paper plates for takeout orders. It was the kind of paper that you might find in a meat market where the butcher behind the counter wrapped freshly cut meat. On the floors in the kitchen area, I noticed these hard black rubber slats; these helped prevent anyone from slipping or falling.

The cold section next to the steam table held coleslaw, potato salad, and condiments like lettuce, tomatoes, pickles, onions, and tartar sauce. On the glass shelves above it, we carried an assortment of pies, which included, at one time or another, Lemon Meringue, Custard, Coconut or Chocolate Cream, Pumpkin, Sweet Potato, and naturally, Apple or Cherry. On the countertop above lay a couple of huge wire racks offering a large variety of snacks: Pretzels, potato chips, Fritos, cheese-flavored popcorn, pork rinses, and others.

The food order counter was just to the right, with an upward-swinging tabletop that would latch onto the side of the cold station. This helped to prevent any customers from stepping out of the front section and into the kitchen area. To the right of the order counter sat this ancient brass cash register with mechanical spring buttons. The top row of buttons showed dollar amounts, and the bottom buttons showed cent amounts. As you pushed down on the selected buttons, the wooden cash drawer would spring open with the ding of a bell. The number of dollars and cents would appear on this glass windowpane atop the cash register.

Under the cash register area were two stainless-steel basins. In one basin, there was a big U-shaped wire brush immersed in soapy water. The second basin had clear water to rinse out glasses before placing them upside down on the drying rack.

Below the order counter and slightly to the upper left of the water basins, you would find a small open compartment. This is where I first laid my eyes on Dad's Colt 45-long barrel pistol tucked away inside the opening. Directly below the order counter was an area with assorted sizes of paper bags for to-go orders. The balance of this area held loaves of wonder bread and round sandwich buns. Once again, a product that came to us from Dad's former employer, Continental Baking Company, which made Wonder Bread and Hostess Cakes.

In front of the cash register was a selection of cigars, boxes of matches, and a stack of business cards. I flipped over one of the business cards and immediately construed my own opinion about Phil Polizzi's sense of humor. On the back of the business card, there was a curvaceous young woman in a polka-dot dress with nylon stockings dangling around her ankles. Above the drawing was this quote, "Barbecue so hot it will knock your socks off."

Behind the cool station was a stove oven, and behind that was a refrigerator. The stove was for cooking barbecue sauce, spaghetti, and spaghetti sauce. The oven for cooking roast beef and pork, along with meatballs. Across from the refrigerator was a metal top grill for cooking hamburgers and grilled cheese sandwiches. To the left of the grill, there was a small yellow prep table.

To the right of the grill was a small storage room area for keeping product items used to service the needs of the restaurant. The room included a back door that flowed into our concrete backyard. Behind and to the left of the grill were two cooking fryers, one bigger than the other. Inside the fryers was hot grease from melted lard. Each fryer contained two wire baskets. The fryers were for cooking fried chicken, a variety of fried fish, and French fries. Next to the cooking fryers was a large, heavy metal prep table with a two-inch thick wood tabletop. This table included a back shelf attached to the tabletop for additional restaurant necessities and, under the table, a lower metal shelf the same size as the tabletop.

Across from this prep table was a chest freezer with six sections, all filled with frozen food products. Above the freezer was open wooden shelving used to store other needed items. To the right side of the freezer was a large pizza oven with no windows. Inside the oven were two shelves, each shelf deep enough to fit two pizzas, one behind the other. On top of the oven lay a paddle with a long handle for reaching into the back part of the pizza oven. This pizza oven sat on top of a long L-shaped prep table used for the preparation of pizzas.

On the right side of this prep table sat one machine for slicing and another machine for grinding. Above the table was more needed shelf space. On this end of the building and to the right of the prep table was an enormous stainless-steel refrigerator that contained two large top and bottom doors and one full-length door.

Across from the pizza area was another large sink area for cleaning pots, pans, dishes, silverware, and other utility cooking products. There was a window above the sink where you could view a portion of the backyard area. To the left of the sink, I spotted an additional door that led into the backyard.

During my first year inside the restaurant, there were times when I would become "Dad's shadow," standing off to one side of him. I would watch his every move, from his waiting on customers to preparing the food orders and then taking their cash. I cannot count the number of times Dad turned around and, taking one step, would land on one of my feet from me being too close. "Why are you on top of me?" he questioned angrily, seeming a bit irritated over my constant shadowing of him. At that point, I knew it was time to back off and stay out of his way.

Since I was not yet old enough to contribute from a work standpoint, I would try to keep busy in other ways. Normally, I would head to the right corner of the main dining room and watch television on the black and white screen. Sometimes, there would be customers already watching a program that did not appeal to me. Whenever that happened, I would start talking and bothering other employees until they asked me to stop.

Nancy, our fry cook, worked on Fridays and Saturday nights. She had a son named Vito, whom I believed to be around thirteen or fourteen years old. He physically possessed the body of a big, heavy, fully-grown man, but mentally, he may have been a bit immature. Sometimes, he would come to the restaurant and hang out while his mother worked. I think she might have asked him to keep me entertained. "C'mon with me," he said, and we would make our way into the restaurant's backyard.

Vito and I would stack up these beer boxes and build a makeshift truck bed. Next, we stacked a couple more beer boxes to the front of it; this was to be our truck cab. Then we stepped into the cab of the truck and sat atop the beer boxes.

Back in those days, glass bottles were the main container for beer. Aluminum cans did not even begin to outsell bottles until 1969. The beer bottles came packed in heavy-duty cardboard boxes. The top of the boxes had a two-sided lid that flipped open and closed tightly into these cutouts in the center of the box.

Vito would make believe we were hauling goods down the road in our eighteen-wheeler. He was always the truck driver, and I always rode shotgun. I now laugh at the idea of just how long it took me to figure out what it was we were doing. As for my part, I was going along for the ride.

Vito gave a respectable performance in pretending to be steering a big wheel, pressing down on the gas pedal, and then stepping down on the clutch to change gears. Vito would also make sound effects with his mouth, "VROOM," imitating a truck rolling down the highway, and then "GIRR" sounds for the gears shifting. I must admit it was quite entertaining. He would make a truck stop, and then we would get out and then back in, only to head off down the road again.

Sometimes, he pretended to pull the truck over and start talking to someone. I would have great difficulty understanding what was going on. I just figured this kind of lingo was way over my head. The other slight problem is that this whole charade took place during winter. Both of us wore heavy coats, and Vito was always wearing a beanie, which he never took off his head. There were times when I would be freezing my butt off. However, from my point of view, it was better to freeze than miss all this great entertainment!

(The 3rd Inning)

---1963---

Our fry cook, Nancy, struck me as an incredibly happy and large middle-aged woman. She did not stay on as our fry cook for a great length of time. This woman had other plans and set her sights on becoming a proprietor of her own business. She somehow managed to pull enough money together and opened a small convenience store.

Her departure ended my days of riding shotgun in the backyard with Vito. There were weekend nights hanging out together, when we would stroll around the city neighborhoods and hang out with a couple of his friends. My walks going out with these older boys gave me this sensation of being a big shot.

I managed to get one last opportunity to visit with this family. Riding along with Dad, we stopped by their convenience store to wish them good luck. They were genuinely nice and offered to let me hang around the store with Vito that afternoon. While there, I observed Nancy and her husband busily working on last-minute preparations for their store's grand opening.

Later in the day, Nancy stopped working long enough to make us sandwiches with bologna from their refrigerated case filled with various lunch meats. During the day, I sensed from watching and listening just how happy and proud she felt to take this big step. Nancy had created an opportunity for herself and her family to become more independent by starting up her own business.

The neighborhood surrounding our restaurant was still a heavily populated white area. Most patrons frequenting our restaurant were of the white race. Every so often, a Black person would come into our place, but all their orders were take-out only. In those days, there was this unwritten law that most restaurants only allowed Black customers to order take-out.

Only after the Civil Rights Act passed in July 1964 did most eateries comply with the new law and allow Black customers to dine in. During our first couple of years in the restaurant business, we only had a minimal number of Black customers. They may have felt intimidated or were aware of this so-called custom and never showed real interest or even attempted to dine in.

Segregation was the greatest contributor to the economic downturn and deterioration that occurred in major cities, small neighborhoods, and other areas around this country. Whenever the Black population began entering a white-segregated neighborhood, it would potentially start a chain reaction, and the white population would begin fleeing the area and thus open more available housing. As the Black population continued to grow, the neighborhood income slowly began to decrease. Over time, housing prices started to drop exponentially, allowing persons with even lower incomes to enter. Continued deterioration inside the neighborhood eventually leads to a rise in the crime rate. As the wealth and income of the area continued to decline, you would begin to see businesses closing.

Over the following years, this same scenario would play out in the neighborhood surrounding our restaurant. Dad was naturally concerned that once Black people began dining inside our restaurant, the same thing would occur to our business. All our white customers would start fleeing and move to other dining establishments.

***

During his lifetime, for whatever reason, Dad had somehow become enthralled with big, tall, and large things. His dogs were no exception, and he took great satisfaction in owning big dogs. The first one came to us while living in our brand-new North St. Louis County home. This beautiful-looking dog had golden-colored fur, and I surmise that he must have been part golden retriever. He reminded my dad of the dog who starred in the 1957 Disney movie "Old Yeller," and that became his given name.

Yeller certainly left an impression on me, and it was a "physical" impression. It happened while I was sitting alone in my bedroom directly behind our garage. I distinctly remember thinking to myself that I should go outside and make sure the car keys were not still in the car's ignition. I did this based on a particular kind of behavioral habit my family had formed. Back in those days, my family was never concerned with leaving keys in the car's ignition when running errands somewhere and getting in and out of the car. This caused them to forget the keys in the car after getting home.

I decided to go outside through the back garage door attached to my room. Taking two steps down, I noticed Yeller quietly sitting on the garage floor. As I slowly began to make my way toward the front of the garage, Yeller came up off the floor and jumped on top of me. At the time, I could not have been more than seven years old. The claw from one of his front paws landed just to the left of my eye, cutting the skin wide open. Running back inside, I threw myself on the bed, moaning and groaning with my hand clutched to the side of my face. I lay there bleeding, and within a moment's notice, my mother came rushing into the room. We drove straight to the hospital, where the doctor sewed me up with four or five stitches. To this day, I can still make out the small scar next to my left eye.

Dad never had too much luck when it came to sharing a long life with his dogs. Yeller never made it to four years old, but he was only the first in the line of other dogs that would be coming our way. Fortunately, the restaurant and its backyard would allow him to create a haven for more big dogs. Mom was not a huge fan of pets. She was always a bit of a neat and clean freak and thought animals were dirty. This meant no dogs, big or small, were allowed inside the home.

The first dog to grace our restaurant backyard was this cute, adorable, and loving mutt. Dad named her Rags, and it was because her coat had waves of wild curls. She was one of the luckier dogs who managed to hang around for a long time. I spent hours of my time with Rags. She could always put a smile on my face. For the time being, Dad seemed satisfied with just this one dog, but there would be more to follow.

***

There was one particularly fun-filled event that occurred every few weeks in our restaurant's backyard. I will laughingly refer to it as "The Bonfire." Up till this point, the only big fires I ever noticed Dad building were the ones inside our massive barbecue pit for cooking all those slabs of ribs.

Inside our backyard, he would collect large empty wooden crates that came with our purchase of fresh chicken halves packed inside of ice. After breaking down these empty wooden crates into pieces, Dad would toss them into this exceptionally large empty oil drum and set the wood on fire. He would then begin adding empty cardboard boxes into the fire one at a time, creating this high-raging fire inside the drum. Sometimes, the fire would reach well above the top of this large oil drum.

When I mentioned these so-called bonfires to my brother Mariano, he jokingly asked, "Didn't you know that Dad was a pyromaniac?" I kept thinking one of these days, a neighbor was going to call the fire department on us. I kept waiting and listening for the sounds of sirens and horns, but miraculously, they never occurred. Fortunately for us, the fires never got out of hand, and Dad's backyard bonfires continued to rage on for years to come.

***

Our restaurant's three waitresses, Laverne, Bee, and Sonja, were all former employees of Phil Polizzi. Sometimes, during the summer, I would go with Mom to our restaurant in the mornings. Laverne would come in shortly thereafter to help with the food preparation and get everything ready for opening.

Laverne looked to be somewhere in her forties, if not older. She was of medium height with platinum blond hair. A heavy smoking habit could well have been the cause of a very raspy-sounding voice. Her darkly tanned skin may have been the evidence and reasoning for it being quite wrinkly.

In my observation of Laverne, I held to the belief that she loved her old boss, Phil. This appeared more obvious to me after hearing about the way he always sweet-talked his lovely waitresses. She had been one of his very loyal employees. My dad was more your no-nonsense and just get-the-job-done kind of guy. You were unlikely to hear any sweet or flowery words coming from his tongue. He did not exactly fall under Laverne's definition of a model employer. However, she thoroughly enjoyed being around my mother. This may have been the one big reason she stayed with us for so long.

Our night waitress, Bee, was an attractive woman with a happy and bubbly personality. She was younger than Laverne and always had a big smile on her face. I liked her very much, as she did me, and one of the things we had in common was baseball. One day, she announced to me, "I am good friends with the man whose job is posting up numbers on the big scoreboard at Busch Stadium." Back then, all the scoreboards at baseball stadiums were manual. Therefore, at least one person needed to take charge and manage the scoreboard. During the home game, their job was to change or update the board by placing these huge, printed numbers up on it. This took place with each half-inning of every ball game played that day.

Busch Stadium was the home of the St. Louis Cardinals. "Oh, Wow, that's got to be a cool job," I surmised. She then asked me something, which caught me completely by surprise. "How would you like me to see if I can arrange for you to get a baseball signed by all the Cardinal baseball players?" I stood there flabbergasted and giddy with joy at the thought of this prospect, but it felt surreal, and skepticism seeped into my brain. "Are you kidding me? Yes, that would be great," I enthusiastically answered her.

As time passed, I impatiently waited with great expectation, hoping this offer of hers would become a reality. From that day on, I would go into the restaurant and anxiously wait for Bee to show up in the evening. "Did you get the ball?" I would question her. "Nope, not yet," she would reply. This conversation went on for weeks while I tried to be continuously optimistic that today would be the day. It was not all that long before the day finally arrived, and Bee walked in wearing an exceptionally large smile on her face.

She handed the ball over to me. I do not think you could have found a happier boy at that moment. It also gave her immense joy to see the look on my face. Bee then said to me, "My friend took this ball into the clubhouse and had every player individually sign it." I kept staring at the ball all day long and looking repeatedly at the handwritten on the ball by the players in the clubhouse. There were the names of Stan Musial, Bob Gibson, Lou Brock, Curt Flood, Ken Boyer, Julian Javier, Bill White, and everyone else on the team.

Right along with my entire family, I had no idea, nor did I realize or appreciate what was in my possession. It sat on a big chest of drawers in the bedroom shared with my three brothers. Understand, I was ten years old and not the brightest little kid in the world, or the neighborhood, for that matter. Not to mention that no one truly explained or gave me advice on the importance or relevance of this ball.

We should have immediately put this collectible into a ball case to preserve the signatures. Then, it would have been untouched by human hands. At the same time, I still would be able to look at the ball and view all those future legendary players.

My understanding or responsibility in owning a collectible item was unclear to me. One of the sadder and more regrettable days in my life would occur shortly thereafter.

I suppose it was not enough for me to merely look at this ball. Besides that, it was the only real baseball I had ever owned. I did not think or even consider asking my parents to buy me another baseball to use for playing. Instead, I started playing with the autographed ball. The signatures on my ball were already slightly beginning to fade. That alone should have told me something.

Then, one day, in my front yard, I happened to be throwing the ball around either by myself or with a friend. It somehow got away from me and started heading down the curbside. Before I could reach my baseball, it went diving down into the street's drainage sewer system.

I was too big to get through the sewer opening, so my next thought was to lift the sewer lid and try to locate the ball. I managed to get the lid off and looked down into a deep, dark hole. I cannot even recall whether the ball was visible. The bottom of the sewer was very dark and very deep. The prospect of me trying to retrieve or somehow climb down into the sewer was outside my exploratory realm of thinking or doing.

I am not, nor have I ever been, one of those courageous individuals fearless enough to explore or dive into unknown spaces. My best and only shot would have been to try and get help from one of my older brothers. Feeling embarrassed for having done such a stupid thing, I must have been more willing to give up the ball rather than admit my blunder. This was not one of my finer moments. I do not wish to think or analyze the reasoning for my lack of attitude in trying to retrieve this ball.

I am not sure if anyone even knew or cared about what happened to that ball. I certainly had no intention of bringing it up. It is quite possible somewhere down the line, the subject of this ball might have come up. As with other things in my life, I may have simply erased any ensuing embarrassment from my memory.

***

During our early years at the restaurant, there were times when we would get a very late-night crowd on Fridays and Saturdays right before closing time. A good portion of this crowd came from a couple of bars in the neighborhood. After a long night of drinking, these people were desperately in need of something to eat. We were not only the closest but the only restaurant in the area still open that late at night. At times, this crowd would become quite loud, and a potential fight might break out.

Before anything too wild could happen, like a flash, Dad would jump in between the fighters like a referee. He abruptly shouted out the command, "You wanna fight? Then, take it outside." Remarkably, it would usually end right there. As I previously mentioned, Dad was fearless and a bit crazy, so neither the situation nor risk mattered much to him. Somehow or someway, people must have sensed or known better than to mess with the man. It could also have been God or one of his guardian angels, always keeping a close watch over him.

Aside from all that, there was one other thing about him that I discovered at an early age. Yes, I realize the man was my father, and other children have made these types of comments about their parents. However, there truly was something vastly different about the look of his eyes. Whenever I got out of line or did anything wrong, he unleashed a look that darted straight through me. Without fail, each time it happened, I immediately felt an immediate sense of fear overcome me and the presence of a threatening evil. Straightening right up, I prepared and braced myself for the worst that might be coming next. The funny thing is nothing else happened. He spotted the look of fright on my face, and that was enough to stop him.

I do not know what happened or how he came to develop that evil stare. It may well have been during those experiences with his father in the tavern and the bootleg liquor business. Dad rarely spoke of those days, and he only said enough for me to know it was a very seedy and unpleasant work environment. In his later years of life, the stare was rarely visible and became almost non-existent.

After the late bar crowd finally cleared out, all the employees worked to finish cleaning up and taking apart everything that needed putting away. It would be 3:30 a.m. or later before we got out of the place. Every so often, Dad would offer to take his few employees out to breakfast at the Toddle house on Lindell Boulevard. One or two of them usually agreed to meet us there. Everyone usually ordered the waffles, but Dad always got an egg order.

Afterward, Dad and I would get back into our car and drive up to this magnificent-looking structure. It is known as College Church and sits on the St. Louis University campus at Grand Avenue and Lindell Boulevard. We were going there to attend the early 5:00 a.m. Sunday morning mass. After that first time and every week thereafter, I would ask if we could go there again. Since I always managed to grab at least a couple of hours of snooze time in one of the booths late on Saturday night, it did not bother me one bit to stay up and go to church.

Of course, it never even crossed my mind how tired Dad must have been. For that matter, why would he even consider doing this after putting in a 14-hour shift at the restaurant?

Through all those long weekend nights into the early morning hours, there were times when Dad would appease my wishes. Sometimes, we attended the 5:00 a.m. mass at College Church. Other times, we would just stop by the 24-hour Mister Donut on our way home. At least once every weekend, he would stop, and I always get one of the Texas donuts. It was about three times the size of a regular glaze donut, but I never had a problem eating the whole thing. Often, he would take home a dozen donuts for the family to enjoy that morning.

There was this one time when Dad really did go beyond expectations. I had kept asking him to go to this 24-hour bowling alley on the way home. One night after closing, he finally did take me there. I thought we had a fun time. What I failed to understand is that Dad really had no time for this kind of fun. It turned out to be a one-time-only deal, and I could not convince him to ever do it again.

***

Grandma Catherine had grown well into the eighties, and her health was failing. Mom no longer felt comfortable leaving my youngest brother, Rio, by himself with her on weekdays. Everyone else in the family was either in school or at work. So, until he started first grade, Mom decided to bring him along with her to the restaurant in the morning.

On their morning drive into the city, they first encountered what our family called "The Halls Ferry Circle." This was the only roundabout in the St. Louis area and one of very few in the country. Even to this day, they are not at all common, with only around 7,000 across the whole country. However, the infamous "Circle" was not your standard roundabout. It had to be big enough to manage the six incoming roads and six outgoing roads that surrounded it. On top of that, all the roads connecting to the circle were main thoroughfares. Whenever traffic on the roadways around the "Circle" was light, it was not too difficult to maneuver in and out. However, the heavier or more congested the roads became, the more dangerous it was to navigate in and out of the circle. When it was busy, this zone was not for the faint of heart. Mom always entered the "Circle" with great care and apprehension.

Along this roundabout was the famous Steak' n Shake, which Mom loved to frequently visit with my sisters. Past this point and moving down the road, they would pass by Velvet Freeze, an old-time favorite ice cream shop. Sometimes, Mom and Rio stopped in there during the rush hour drive home. Passing the ice cream shop during the morning led them onto Broadway Street. At the end of Broadway came a short drive down Highway I-70 over to the Grand Ave exit. Off in the distance, on a sunny day, they could see downtown St. Louis. They would glance over at the St. Louis Skyline to search for any progress on the Gateway Arch under construction and going up along the Mississippi Riverfront in the downtown area. The Gateway Arch was built to commemorate President Thomas Jefferson's Louisiana Purchase of 1803 and to celebrate St. Louis's significant role in the rapid westward expansion that followed. The inception of this monument began in 1933. However, it was not until February of 1963 that construction started on this 630-foot high and wide stainless-steel monument.

Exiting the highway onto Grand Avenue, they passed by an old St. Louis landmark called "The Water Tower." Rio asked Mom about this place, and she told him, "This was a place where they used to water the horses around here. The Water Tower, built back in 1871, had an architectural form that was that of a Corinthian order column with brick stone and cast-iron trim. It stands 154 feet tall. In addition to its use for firefighting, the pressure in the pipe regulated water pressure in the area. In 1912, they decommissioned it.

Their last stop of the morning was at the bank to make a deposit or get more coins for making change. Since he was under six years of age, Rio could not be of any real help at the restaurant. Like me, he enjoyed playing in the backyard with our dog, Rags. He would pass the time enjoying our restaurant food, drinking soda, and playing the jukebox. Sometimes, he walked down the block to a mom-and-pop store for penny candy. Rio considered himself lucky to be there and enjoyed having all that food, soda, and all the fun he had before he started first grade.

Around this time, our night waitress, Bee, decided it was time to move on. Dad's replacement for her would become our most loyal employee. Mary Stephens came to work for us and stayed up till the restaurant's end. She was a very tall, thin, dark-haired lady who must have been somewhere around 40 years of age. She divorced her husband early in their marriage after he walked away, leaving her with three young boys to support.

Mary was a good woman, but she did have one little thing quirky about her appearance: she was a bit hairy. A couple of my siblings laughed about the hair that grew above her lip, but I ignored them, figuring they were just having playful fun. I knew how my siblings, me included, could get a little mean with our jabs and barbs, but we loved teasing one another. There were times when we all may have crossed the line. The thing is, we learned never to take the teasing too seriously, and thankfully, we never allowed it to become an issue between us.

Shortly after hiring Mary Stephens, her eldest son came to work for us. Art came in on the weekends, and his job was making pizzas and washing the dishes, pots, and pans. During the week, he attended a junior college and majored in accounting. The family lived in Pine Lawn, a mixed community of Black and white people. For them, it was a necessary and economically lower-priced part of the town.

Mary happened to be one of those individuals who never learned to drive a car. She would take the bus every day to work. Our restaurant stayed open much later than her bus ran at night. Dad felt very strongly about employing this woman. He understood and somehow knew she could be someone to count on to come in every night to do her job. For this reason, he was willing to go out of his way and give her a ride home.

We also employed a part-time waitress, Sonja. This young woman was quite outspoken, usually a little too much for her own good. This was Phil Polizzi's daughter-in-law, who had married his oldest son, Vince. They moved into the house next door to our restaurant after Phil had moved out. The couple also had an adorable two-year-old daughter.

There was one thing I always wondered about this little girl, and that was her real first name. As far as I could tell, "Cutie" was the only name she ever went by. The idea that this was her real name was utterly confusing to me. I came across this same predicament with one of my childhood friends who

lived on the corner of my street. His little sister also went by
an unusual first name, "Sweetie."

Although I never really did figure out if these were the
two girls' real names, it certainly left me with something to
think about.

***

Around this same period, I discovered something quite
unexpected on one fateful Saturday afternoon. There was not
much going on inside the restaurant, and we were simply
enjoying a brief period of peace and quiet. Dad and I were
sitting at one of the booths. His back was to the clock, which
hung high above the cash register area. He then asked me,
"What time is it?" I stood up and looked at the clock and then
began moving closer and closer in that direction. After reaching
within ten feet or so of the clock face, I announced the time.

Dad turned around and, looking in my direction, asked
me an interesting question. "Why did you find it necessary to
walk all the way over there and get that close to the clock to
tell me the time?" To my surprise, I had never really given it
any thought. Others may have overlooked this sign completely,
but Dad was very observant of his children and sharp enough
to realize this was abnormal behavior for a person with good
vision. At that moment, he understood I might need corrective
vision.

My suspicion is when you are younger, and it is likely
you do not realize how good a person's long-range vision is
supposed to be. Clear vision was not my problem. It was seeing
clearly from a greater distance and not knowing whether my
eyesight qualified as 20-20 vision. Besides that, if you do not
have a problem seeing and no one else observes it, how does
one know?

72

I am not sure why, but at first, I thought glasses were something cool to wear. Shortly thereafter, I concluded they were an obstacle, hindrance, nuisance, and inconvenience. Nowadays, there are so many more options and types of contact lenses or even surgery. In my situation, and during that time, glasses were my only choice.

***

Our busiest day of the week at the restaurant was Fridays, with one major reason contributing to this fact. The Catholic church required its members to abstain from eating meat on Fridays. (In 1966, No Meat Fridays changed to No Meat Fridays only during the Lent season). Also, there happened to be a Catholic church and school, St. Augustine, only a couple of blocks from our restaurant. Based on the number of fish we sold on Friday and the location of the church, it seemed quite likely the area around our restaurant was heavily concentrated with members of the Catholic faith.

The two main fish sandwiches and dinner plates we sold were Filet of Sole and Jack Salmon. The filets came to us, breaded and frozen. The Jack Salmon was also frozen, but for this fish, we added breading. We cooked both kinds of fish in our large deep fryers. The filet was boneless and put between two pieces of bread with a side of pickles and onions.

For those unfamiliar with the term Jack Salmon, it is a skinny, foot-long, batter-fried, bone-in, tail-on finfish. Bone-in fish tend to be moist and more flavorful than fillets, and the whiting pulls very easily off the firm, hard bone. Technically, a "jack" is a male salmon that returns to spawn one year sooner than other adult salmon and, therefore, is smaller in size.

The cooked Jack Salmon lay atop two slices of bread with pickles and onion. There was also another tantalizing reason behind the great demand for these two fish orders on Friday. "Pour some of that barbecue sauce over my fish," customers requested. Our customers enjoyed the taste of Phil's "so-called" famous barbecue sauce on top of their fried fish.

The Friday evening rush required us to carry one additional employee. Dad could not afford to pay for another employee. So, during that first year of business, the answer was to recruit my two oldest brothers for assistance in the Friday evening dinner rush. They were both already working full-time jobs, but they knew better than to refuse his request.

Mom would stay there working until 8:00 p.m. On the day before, she would bring home something from our restaurant for us to cook on Friday nights. We got something like breaded shrimp or the fixings for a cheese pizza. It was normally just the younger children and our grandmother for dinner.

We missed our mom not being there on those nights. No matter the number of things or problems she might be juggling, we could always count on her to bring happiness and ease into our home. Not to mention, we hated watching our grandmother moaning and complaining about her daughter not being there. My three youngest sisters were 16, 13, and 8, with little experience cooking. Dinners would not always come out all that great, and Grandma would show off her displeasure with the meals.

When my sister Lucia was fourteen years old, Mom arrived home one day from the restaurant with news. "Your father wants you to help out with the Friday evening dinner rush," she reported. My two oldest brothers were no longer available to pitch in, and Dad needed a replacement. Lucia quickly realized she could now say goodbye to any other plans on Friday nights.

The following week, Lucia arrived at the restaurant ready to go to work. Dad instructed her on how to operate our ancient cash register. From the look of this machine, it may have been in use since the turn of the century. Her other duties were filling cups with coleslaw and potato salad for the fish dinners. She was also in charge of cleaning all the dirty glasses from the dining room crowd.

Like all the rest of us children, Lucia had always been a bit afraid of our dad. However, she noticed that Dad was treating her surprisingly well. Whenever there was a lull during the Friday evening rush, Dad instructed her to take a seat, sit down, and relax. Within moments, our waitress, Mary, would come over and start talking to her. Lucia got concerned that the waitress might be neglecting her dining room customers. So, instead of sitting down, she would normally just stay put at the cash register counter. Dad would cheer her up, saying, "You bring me good luck because when you're here on Fridays, we get lots of customers."

Whenever a young man came in for a carryout order and appeared to be looking too closely or intently at Lucia, Dad stepped up to the counter with their order. "I will take care of this one," he announced while staring them down at the same time. She thought it was funny because they would hand over the money, grab their order, and then hustle out the door.

***

There happened to be this one other thing that really got under Dad's skin. This would occur much later in the evening on Friday nights, long after Mom and Lucia returned home. A group of young teenage boys would start coming into the place around 10 p.m. As they walked in, Dad would immediately direct them into the small dining cove area and away from the main dining room. This served a dual purpose, allowing him to keep a watchful eye on them in one place and to avoid a disturbance to other dining customers. They chose to congregate around our place with the sole purpose of making it their Friday night hangout.

The first thing they would do is purchase a bottle of soda pop from our large chest refrigerator in the front section of the restaurant. Boys that had a little extra money would also purchase an order of French fries. One time, a boy asked for barbecue sauce over his fries. At first, Dad freely went along with this request. Eventually, they all started wanting barbecue sauce on their fries, so he started charging them five or ten cents extra for it.

These boys could tend to get a little too loud. Of course, whenever they began getting too rowdy, Dad shut them down immediately. Overall, they were quite harmless, but among the whole lot of them, they spent less than five dollars. Sometimes, they would stick around for an hour or two. At times, it could be a bit amusing to watch and listen to their playful antics, but at the same time, I understood Dad's frustration with these boys.

Around this time, Dad must have figured the time had come for me to start getting my feet wet into the business. He believed I was this math whiz or prodigy. From an incredibly early age and before ever attending school, I had this automatic ability to add and subtract numbers in my head. I recall this one instance when my Uncle Steve and his family came over to our home for a visit. Dad started bragging to his younger brother about my math prowess.

Uncle Steve called me over to him and gripped my hands. He squeezed my fingers as tightly as possible. He believed that I was using my fingers to calculate the answers. My uncle was trying to expose me as being some kind of phony. However, I passed his addition and subtraction problems flawlessly. These tests caused me to wonder if my uncle did this due to his non-belief or a bit of jealousy.

My very first restaurant assignment was to keep the drinking glasses thoroughly clean. All dirty glasses were set down on a tray stand by two basins of water below the cash register area. My job was to dip each glass into a basin of soapy water and then place it over this U-shaped brush. I ended up turning this job into a game by moving the glass up and down extremely hard and quickly over the soapy brush, generating an overabundance of suds. Then, I rinsed each glass in the basin filled with clear water before placing it on the tray stand.

The next thing was to prove that I could manage the cash register. Dad wanted to see me put my mathematical skills to work. I patiently watched for customers to step up out of the dining room, walk past the long steam table, and over to the cash register area to pay their bills. My job was to stand there with a smile on my face and my hand out, waiting for them to hand over their bill and payment. I would first look at the bill and then announce the amount to collect.

In the beginning, I received a fair amount of surprised and strange looks from customers. It obviously was not an everyday occurrence to see a young boy the age of ten years old taking money and making change. Customers might have wondered or at least been a bit skeptical about how accurate this young boy was going to be at managing their money. However, I always put their fears to rest after handing them back the correct change. Sometimes, I got a kick out of seeing the expression on their faces when they handed me their bill.

Also, the look of surprise or amazement at how quickly and accurately I gave them back their change. On rare occasions, they would hand me a small tip. Not only was it a rare treat, but it never failed to give me a good, happy feeling.

Admittedly, there was one type of calculation that I found to be quite perplexing. To this day, I cannot understand why it was so difficult for me to figure this one out. Let us say the bill was $4.25. If they handed me a five-dollar bill and one quarter, I easily understood they were looking to get one dollar back. That was easy, yet there was this one common instance from the very keen money handlers that would throw me. It was my first stint at making change, and this one calculation seemed a bit too sophisticated and complicated for me.

Here is an example of how this conundrum would occur. Let us say the bill was $4.32, and the customer handed me a five-dollar bill and seven cents. This type of calculation would throw me off. I understood they had sixty-eight cents coming back from the five-dollar bill, but I did not comprehend the purpose of them giving me the extra seven cents. It really should not have been that difficult to figure out. In the future, newer cash registers will calculate these numbers for you. I was dealing with a manual cash register and did everything in my head. I never considered or thought to simply take $5.07 minus $4.32 = .75 cents. Their purpose for handing me a five-dollar bill and adding seven cents was to get back three quarters to cut back on the amount of small loose change.

Fortunately, this embarrassment only happened on rare occasions and a handful of times before I finally figured it out with a little help from Dad. When looking back, it is amazing to me that my father put so much faith and trust in me to manage the cash register. At first, I had supposed he just thought I was good at calculating numbers and money. Then it hit me: he had done the same thing when running his father's grocery store when he was my age.

At least for now, this would be the extent of my work contribution, and that was good enough for me. I thoroughly enjoyed being around my father and watching all the activities going on in and around the restaurant. I particularly enjoyed watching Dad work on the take-out orders for customers, observing his every move and how quickly he prepared their food orders.

Whenever there was a slowdown in business, I would grab the opportunity to take a break. I might take a seat and watch something on television, but sometimes, customers would be watching something of no interest to me. So then, I might go into our backyard and play with our dog, Rags, or take a short stroll around the neighborhood.

Every so often, I managed to convince Dad to give me permission to walk over to the Northside Theater and catch a double feature. If the St. Louis Cardinals were in town, I would sometimes try to get permission to see a baseball game all by myself. Oh yes, and make no mistake, I very much enjoyed eating all the variety of foods that our restaurant had to offer. This became even more satisfying when I finally got the chance to prepare my own food and make it exactly the way I liked it.

Dad allowed me quite a bit of freedom to roam around, as much as I pleased, during those first couple of years. He was not very dependent upon me being there working all the time. If it was not too busy, I might take a walk around the neighborhood and go exploring. We had four mom-and-pop convenience stores, all within blocks of each other. I would always go out with a purpose in mind. For example, picking up something Mom or Dad needed from the convenience store, either for themselves or the restaurant.

A couple of these mom-and-pop shops had one of my new favorite toys, a pinball machine. This electronic gadget was something different. I had never experienced anything like this before, unlike today, where there are innumerable kinds of electronic gadgets and games to play. I became fascinated and captured by all the flickering lights and various kinds of sounds coming out of these machines. To play one game cost me a nickel. Having never played, I was not particularly good at the game, and one nickel did not go far or last too long.

Sometimes, the choice was to buy something with my money or play pinball games and, within a matter of minutes, have nothing to show for it. Even so, these pinball machines could be addictive. I never imagined this was only an initial phase into the eventual video game craze. Every so often, I would get the urge to put a nickel or two in the machine, always with the hope and expectation of winning additional games and the chance to play longer.

I also liked to spend part of my time at these shops checking out the selection of penny candy. This consisted of items like Tootsie Rolls, Bit-O-Honey, candy buttons, candy necklaces, peppermints, Pixy Stix, Mary Janes, Bottle Caps, Tootsie Pops, chocolate coins, gum balls, licorice sticks, Atomic Fireballs, and more.

Another thing I enjoyed buying, as much as the candy, was a fresh pack of baseball trading cards. I have always loved baseball and had a great interest in the statistics on the back of these cards. For a bonus, there would be this huge stick of bubble gum in each pack. Sometimes, the gum inside of the pack of cards was hard and stale. This normally occurs if the packs stay on the store shelf for too long. Of course, I would chew the gum up, anyway.

I carefully went through every baseball card to try and memorize the statistics of each player. Another step in my process was grouping each player's card into their respective teams. I kept every team separated by placing a tight rubber band around each one of them. One of the bigger cigar boxes sitting on our cash register stand had gone empty. I quickly grabbed it and put all my cards in this box for safekeeping.

Another business one block down the street from our restaurant was a hardware store. This place offered absolutely no interest to me. I have never had any type of affinity for working with tools in fixing or building things. There would be times when Dad sent me over to this store to pick up an item for him. With a little bit of luck, I could usually find what he needed.

Across the street from the hardware store was something of greater interest to me. This would become another of my favorite places to visit. The neighborhood dairy store became my place of choice for purchasing soft-serve ice cream. Without fail, I visited there once every weekend to purchase a banana split.

Incidentally, their creation was not your standard presentation of this novelty treat. Instead of your basic banana boat, they simply used a very tall cup. The soft serve ice cream went into the bottom of the cup and topped with chocolate syrup; then, more soft serve ice cream with strawberry topping; next, four pieces of a banana inside of the cup; then, more soft serve ice cream with pineapple topping. Lastly, the whipped cream and crushed nuts, with a cherry on top.

Although it may not have been my preferred choice of presentation for this treat, the taste alone was satisfying enough for me. Besides that, it was so practical. I could ask for a lid, place it in our restaurant freezer, and have it for dessert anytime I wanted after my dinner. It is one example of my measured and calculated habits. Also, it offered an indication of my early days with an obsession with sweets.

One weekend, Dad produced a plan and procedure on how we would be exiting the building at closing time. Right before we prepared to leave, he approached me with the following instructions, "Open the cash register, take out all the cash, and place it into this bank bag." Next, I was handed three Styrofoam coffee cups with lids. "Put all the loose change, nickels, dimes, and quarters inside these cups and put them in the bank bag," he instructed. After that, he directed me to put the bank bag into one of the brown or white paper bags we used for take-out orders. I assumed this was to camouflage the bank bag. The real problem is we did not have a safe where we could keep the money. Besides, Dad certainly was not taking any chance of someone breaking into the place overnight and cleaning out the cash register.

As we prepared to leave the building, Dad reached under the cash register counter and put his hand into the open compartment to retrieve his Colt 45 long-barrel gun. He then proceeded toward the front door with the gun by his side. Unlocking the front door entrance and stepping outside, he instructed us to wait inside for a moment. After taking a quick look around and surveying the area, Dad would give our waitress, Mary, and me the good-to-go signal. We both made our way to the car while he locked up behind us.

Oh yes, I forgot one minor detail. Dad left me holding the bag. What I mean to say is that he put me in charge of holding the money bag. The problem with this is all those closing preparations and tactics had now scared the poop out of me. I started imagining there might be this big shootout occurring to get our money. So, what do I do? Even though the car was less than a hundred feet away, I made a run for it.

Making his way toward the car, Dad opened his car door on the driver's side, stepped in, and blurted out at me, "What the hell are you running for?" I thought to myself, seriously? Why am I running? Then, shyly but defiantly, I replied to him, "I wasn't running."

This same routine went on every night at closing for the following years to come. No matter how hard I tried, I could not help myself, and the absolute best I could do was a fast walk. And without fail, Dad would get into the car and sometimes, with sympathy in his voice, ask me the same question, "Why are you running?" And he would always get the same answer, "I'm not running."

***

The first of my siblings was now engaged to be married. Patricia's one and only long-term dream of finding her prince to marry someday was finally here. Of course, every family with deep Italian roots has a big traditional wedding for their daughters.

Owning the restaurant allowed our parents to be their own caterers. For the wedding shower, they decided to close the restaurant for one afternoon. My sister Patricia will never forget that day. She walked into the restaurant and spotted our relatives, her fiancée's relatives, and her friends, all sitting around the tables and shouting, "Surprise." She was in shock and amazement at the number of people who showed up for her bridal shower.

Mom searched long and hard before finally locating a large wedding hall for a very reasonable price, especially considering its date, the first day of June. Our parents catered for the wedding and, with a little help, did all the cooking and then served the food to approximately three hundred guests. After dinner was over, they were finally able to get the chance to visit with their guests and enjoy the balance of their daughter's wedding. At the end of the day, Mom and Dad were ecstatic because what truly mattered was that they had accomplished giving their first daughter a big and beautiful wedding day.

***

Sundays at home with all my family were the absolute best of times. It was the only day of the week with a decent chance everyone might be home for afternoon dinner. On Sundays, it was a family tradition to have pasta with sauce and some kind of meat. Occasionally, Mom would make us her special homemade pasta, and if she got ambitious, homemade ravioli. Otherwise, it would be a choice between mostaccioli, pasta shells, or plain spaghetti.

The pasta would usually include meatballs, sausage, chuck steak, or chicken. I loved them all because Mom simmered the meat inside of her homemade pasta sauce. There was nothing better than when she took a piece of bread, spooned a little sauce over it, and handed it to me.

We would add two extra leaves to the table so all thirteen of us could squeeze around the table. Everyone ate off regular plates except Dad; his portion of pasta was set on a platter. Sunday dinners were early afternoon, and then later in the day, our big treat would be a bowl of Jell-O, usually cherry or strawberry flavored, with banana slices. Sometimes, in place of bananas, Mom would add a can of fruit cocktail.

I remember Dad giving me an account of the family dinners when he was a young boy. "We would have spaghetti for dinner every night served with a different vegetable, no meat. The only time we ever got meat was on Sunday, and that was a big treat," he recalled.

During the summer months, Mom would prepare all kinds of fruit for canning. She would store them in glass mason jars. She would buy a bushel of peaches and pears, then peel them and cut them in half for preparation and storage. One thing I craved was the plum preserves that she bottled. I loved putting this stuff on pancakes she made from scratch. Her biggest canning was that of tomatoes. She canned enough jars to last for an entire year. On Sundays, Mom would go downstairs and grab a couple of jars from the canned goods shelves. These jars were the main ingredient for her spaghetti sauce.

Every couple of months, on Sunday evenings, we younger children would go along with Mom and Dad for get-togethers with our uncles and aunts at one of their homes. I would immediately gravitate my way over to my cousins and spend my time playing with them. My favorite cousins were two brothers around the same age as me, Donnie and Nicky. In the summertime, the three of us would take turns and spend a week together at each other's family.

As much as I loved traditional Sunday dinners with the entire family, it was nothing compared to our Christmas holidays. The spirit of the holiday season with all of us being together, our strong bond, and our great love for one another warmed my heart like nothing else did. Our brother Nick took charge of operating the newly purchased 8mm movie camera. For all holidays to come, we would take turns videotaping the family for posterity. We mostly videotaped all of us hanging around the Christmas tree, and at other times, we sat around our large dinner table enjoying all the delicious cookies and pastries that Mom had prepared. Eventually, I would take charge of the video duties after Nick left home and entered the army.

About two months before Christmas, Mom would begin making trays and trays of Christmas cookies, mostly Italian. One of my favorites was the Cuccidati, a thin pie crust cookie dough filled with a recipe containing ground-up figs and other spices. After baking, a white icing goes over the cookie, with candy sprinkles. I can guarantee you that this cookie puts the fig Newton to shame.

Another one of my favorites was the sliced cookies. This was a smaller version of today's Biscotti cookies. Mom would add just the right amount of candied fruit and almonds to the dough. It came out of the oven looking like a cookie loaf, which she then sliced up and placed back into the oven for toasting. There was another Italian cookie where the dough had the shape of a long, skinny snake. It then goes into a tray of sesame seeds before cutting it up into smaller pieces for baking. There were certain other kinds of Italian-style cookies, along with red and green Christmas tree-pressed cookies, snowballs, and chocolate chips.

Then, right before the holidays arrived, Mom would make three marvelously delicious Italian pastries. The first one is the Sfingi, a light, hollow, fried pastry topped with honey and crushed nuts or sprinkled with sugar. The second one is a ravioli pastry filled with a sweet ricotta cheese recipe and semi-sweet chocolate chips mixed inside. This ravioli pastry could also have a chickpea filling, Dad's favorite.

Finally, there was your conventional and most popular of all Italian pastries, the Cannoli. Mom would make these from scratch, too. After making the dough, she would wrap it around these small metal tubes and fry them in oil. A special ricotta cheese cream recipe was the filling for the pastry shell. All three of these pastries would not be on your list for one of your healthiest desserts. However, the taste and pleasure of eating them during the holiday season made it well worth any health risks.

One last traditional family holiday goodie was the chestnut. These are seasonal nuts; they are only available during the fall season. The first thing you must do when preparing chestnuts is to cut a cross into the shell. Since we did not have a special pan for roasting them over an open fire, we used the oven. After coming out of the oven, Dad would wrap them in a large towel. This would trap the steam inside them and soften the inner shell, making it easier to peel the shell away from the nut. I could barely wait for them to cool inside the towel. For me, the taste of biting into this warm, sweet nut added to the magical feel of the holidays. I also loved sprinkling a bit of salt over the nut to enhance the flavor even more.

We would buy chestnuts in time to have a special treat to finish off Thanksgiving dinner. There was one year when my brother Nick had started videotaping us around the table, and then suddenly, a chestnut shell fight broke out. Mom started the fight, but in the end, we ganged up to bombard her with these shells, and she got the worst of it.

As the years pass by, these traditional family favorites have come to mean more than just the mere eating and enjoying them. It has brought a sense of déjà vu and causes me to reminisce about those special holidays with Mom, Dad, Grandma, and all of us children inside our loving, happy family.

***

At our restaurant, Dad would always come into the place dressed in the same attire. He wore this white T-shirt with a pair of pants and then wrapped a long white apron around his waist. In ways, he looked more like a baker than a restaurant owner.

One day, an injury to his lower back was causing him great difficulty in continuing to move in his usual breakneck, speedy manner. He began to wear back braces so that he could move around well enough to work. My older brother, Nick, had recently graduated from high school and had been working to save up money for college. "Come and work for me at the restaurant until I can get around a little better," Dad suggested, "And I will do what I can to help you with college tuition."

Nick began helping part-time at the restaurant, but Dad kept coming in without taking any real time off to allow his back to heal. Within a matter of weeks, the back brace offered him the needed relief, and the back issue diminished. It also became evident there was not going to be any money available to help fund his son's college tuition. Dad released Nick from his restaurant duties so that he could pick up a second job and be able to earn enough money to pay for college tuition.

It was slowly becoming evident that any thoughts or hopes of seeing increased restaurant sales from where they stood were highly unlikely. In truth, sales had already begun showing signs of a slight decline, and demographics in the area and the neighborhood were continuing to change. More middle-class whites were fleeing the area and replaced with lower-income individuals, a good portion of them coming from the Black community.

We could not afford to take a hit on the business income. Soon afterward, Dad decided to start opening the restaurant on Sundays. The entire family was very unhappy and upset with this decision. Although it may have been the last thing he wanted to do, Dad felt he had no other choice in the matter.

When the restaurant began opening on Sundays, we stayed open from noon till 8 p.m. This allowed Dad to still have a brief time in the morning and late evening with the family. Thankfully, Mom would not be going to the restaurant on Sundays. Our waitress, Mary, certainly needed the money and willingly agreed to work those days.

My continuous need to be around my father whenever possible meant deciding if I should give up Sundays at home or my time with him. There were times that I would have preferred to stay home but decided to go with him, sensing he wanted me there. Although he never told me so, I am certain it pleased him to have family around on those days.

Quite often, Dad allowed me to leave for a couple of hours, and I would go over to the Northside movie theater or even a ballgame if the Cardinals were playing in town. One of the things I appreciated most was the fact it was during daylight hours. This allowed me to feel a little more comfortable when taking my longer journeys away from the restaurant by myself.

My sister, Patricia, and her newlywed husband occasionally would come by the restaurant to visit Dad on the weekend. He was always working, and my sister missed seeing him when she would come over to the house to visit us. The couple normally show up at the restaurant around 7 p.m. on Saturday and would find Dad working away at pleasing his customers. The minute he spotted them walking into the place, you could see a smile forming on his face. As Patricia moved closer toward greeting him with a hug and kiss, the smile on his face grew bigger.

After the couple found a seat, Dad would stop and go over to their table and get them something to eat or drink. They would patiently wait until he was completely free and had the time to spend with them. Her husband, Steve, could always get Dad laughing at his jokes, and seeing him feel a bit of enjoyment made Patricia that much happier.

***

There was one customer who befriended me, and it just so happened that his name was the same as mine. Mike was a good-looking, middle-aged man from the Czech Republic. As far as I could tell, he was a single man who never mentioned any wife or family. Besides that, he always came to the restaurant by himself. Based on our conversations, all signs indicated to me that Mike was a bit of a gambler. Our best conversations centered around the subject of baseball. There was just one problem: he was a fan of the Chicago Cubs, and my St. Louis Cardinals were their biggest rivals.

Sometimes, our conversations regarding these two teams would get quite spirited and competitive, but it was all good, playful fun. Our rivalry talks finally came to a head during a weekend when the Cubs were in town to play the Cardinals. He took this opportunity to take advantage of my great fondness for my team and proposed a small wager that leaned in his favor. "I will put up two dollars to your one dollar that the Cardinals do not take both games of today's doubleheader," he proposed. Mike was not willing to take a risk on a single game; however, he was ready to take a risk that the Cubs would win one of two games. I was gung-ho and so confident in my team that I talked Dad into taking the bet.

The Cardinals had won their share of doubleheaders against the Cubs, but this would not be one of those times.

Although the Cardinals did go on to win the second game, they lost the first one. Mike stayed at the restaurant, sitting across from me, as we enjoyed listening to the entire first game. I always wondered if he would have stuck around for the entire second game had the Cardinals won that first one.

To my way of thinking, although Mike won the battle of our bet, he lost the war. In the following year, the St. Louis Cardinals would go on to win the National League pennant and beat the Yankees in the World Series. The Chicago Cubs would wait for more than fifty years before accomplishing this same feat. I would be willing to take the bet that he was not around to see it.

Admittedly, like my friend Mike, I, too, would become a bit of a gambler. I love sports and working with crunching and calculating numbers. For this reason, as I grew older, I became a very avid handicapper of horseracing.

As you may have already noticed, all the names of my siblings came with a specific reason or purpose in mind. In my case, the circumstances were different and random. Mom and Dad could not decide between the names of Michael and Mark, so they placed both names in a hat to determine the outcome of their two choices. Michael won.

Now, there has always been quite a bit of speculation and discussion on the relevance and importance of the naming of a child. There have also been discussions on whether it truly has any effect on the outcome of their future. I have given thought and consideration to the fact my name came to me through chance. So, I cannot help but wonder if my name caused some kind of celestial effect on my desire for chance betting.

***

Before 1963 ended, the people of this country lived through one incredibly sad and shocking event. To this day, it still resonates with the people who remember it.

It was an early Friday afternoon, and my fifth-grade class was lining up to head into the school auditorium. We were preparing to see a film called "Our Mr. Sun." It is a documentary that explains how the sun works and how it also plays a huge part in human life.

Suddenly, over the classroom intercom, we heard the following message from our school principal. "The President of the United States has been shot and is being taken to the hospital," she announced. Immediately, I looked around for my teacher, Miss Thrower. She was a younger woman around thirtyish with bad acne skin condition, very evident by the marks on her face. I noticed tears starting to come streaming down her face, and she turned away, extremely upset. Admittedly, I was a bit surprised and confused by this strong reaction. We were all shocked and upset upon hearing the news, but as far as I knew, this was not a family member or even a close friend of hers.

It was not until later that I was able to understand her reaction to this news. John F. Kennedy was a popular president with the American people. The saying goes that everybody who was around at that time can still exactly remember what they were doing the moment they heard the news. I can certainly agree and attest to that statement.

(The 4th Inning)

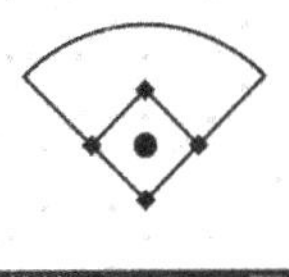

---1964---

Dad could not shake this bug of adding a second dog to the restaurant's backyard. He fixed his sights on locating a Great Dane with a litter of puppies. The purpose of breeding Great Danes was to create boar-hunting dogs in Europe during the 1800s. They are known as the "Apollo of dogs" due to their stately grace. Like other large breeds, they can be susceptible to health issues.

It did not take long before Dad came across a newspaper ad selling a Great Dane litter of puppies. I went along with him to check out the litter. Upon arriving, we discovered there were only two pups still available for sale. One of them was the runt of the litter, and the owners were selling him for less than the other. I now wonder if Dad was taking into consideration his own small stature when choosing to go with the runt.

The term "runt of the litter" describes the smallest or weakest of all the puppies in a dog's litter. Runts are simply puppies who had the misfortune of poor placement in utero while other pups were in a better position. They can have heart defects and other congenital problems, including umbilical hernias, that the breeder might not disclose to you. So, it would be wise to have your veterinarian do a complete examination before you agree to buy the pup.

I suppose Dad might have been ignorant of all these facts and did not completely understand the risk of purchasing a runt. However, it later became clear to me that he was determined to do everything in his power to help this little guy survive. To see him grow bigger and stronger every day would be an extremely rewarding experience.

Little Rico, as we called him, had his ears cropped and would give off the cutest and most adorable looks imaginable. He received the utmost care, and Dad went as far as keeping him in the storage room of the restaurant to keep a special watch over him. Every so often, you could hear a little yelp or bark coming from there. I have no idea what our customers must have thought or wondered when hearing those sounds.

Rico started to blossom and grow till he reached three or four months old. However, it was becoming evident that he must have been born with a medical defect that was causing him to constantly struggle to stay healthy and grow. It just became a matter of time before little Rico would succumb to all his illnesses. Dad and his desire to be the proud owner of a pedigree, stately-graced Great Dane was not meant to be. In time, he would begin a search to find another and even bigger breed of dog.

***

There happened to be this one very strange and unexpected event that occurred early one spring morning outside my home. The family awakened to this blaring sound coming out of the horn of a car. It was our dad's Plymouth

Valiant, an automobile marketed in the United States from 1960 through 1976. The design and building of this vehicle came from the Plymouth corporation as a way to enter the compact car market that emerged during the late 1950s.

The car horn continued blaring out this same unending sound, which I likened to someone screaming they were in dire need of help. Opening the front door of our home, we witnessed fiery flames roaring from the back seat of our car with the rear windows down. I would venture to guess Dad arrived home a couple of hours earlier and, being very tired, failed when attempting to flip his lit cigarette butt out the car window. The lit cigarette butt must have flown into the back seat, and it caught on fire.

Back in those days, the popularity of cigarette smoking in America was bigger than ever. In 1900, on a per capita basis, American adults smoked approximately fifty-four cigarettes per year. The number of cigarettes consumed increased exponentially until its peak in 1963 to an estimated 4345 cigarettes per year. This meant that the consumption of cigarette smoking had remarkably seen an increase of eighty-fold.

Like so many other Americans, Dad enjoyed smoking, beginning with the popular nonfiltered Camel cigarettes before later switching to the longer nonfiltered Pall Mall cigarettes.

Fortunately, we managed to extinguish the car fire quickly. The only damage was to the car's back seat, sent directly into the trash bin. Our car insurance was only for liability coverage. This meant no funds to replace the back seat. Since there was no other real damage to the car, Dad continued driving it without a back seat.

When your car horn takes on a life of its own, it is due to the following reasons: a faulty relay, a short circuit, or a faulty horn push button. The fire was in the back seat of the car. None of the issues mentioned appears to be the case in this situation. This horn going off may well have saved us from losing our car altogether. Therefore, the question remains: Why did this car horn begin blaring non-stop once the fire began?

On the weekends after closing, Dad drove our waitress, Mary, to her home. This meant I got stuck sitting on the floorboard in the back of the car. I can guarantee you this was not a pleasant ride or experience. The floorboard that I sat upon was anything but comfortable, and it tended to get extremely warm. The ride would also be quite bumpy. After growing quite tired of this routine, an idea occurred to me. I grabbed one of the sturdy beer cases from the backyard where Vito and I used to concoct our so-called eighteen-wheeler rides. If nothing else, the beer case saved me from riding on an uncomfortable floorboard.

It is possible that Dad eventually did locate a back seat from a local junkyard. However, all I can remember was those awful rides in the back of that car. Thankfully, the day came when we finally traded it in for another car.

***

During the first weekend in June 1964, my brother Don took the plunge into marriage with his bride, Suzanne Cundiff. The chosen venue for their reception party was Le Chateau, a stylishly luxurious and expensive facility located in Frontenac. This area of town was the residence of wealthier people in the St. Louis metropolitan area.

My Grandpa Damiano had a brother named Steve. All his children went through a formal education, and his sons became doctors, dentists, and pharmacists. Grandpa Damiano's children were either sent off to a trade school or simply dropped out of the educational system, just like Dad. These cousins were good people, but this group had one glaring and disrespectful tendency of wanting to keep my family within our class of economic standing.

There were comments, such as, my brother had no business having a reception at Le Chateau. When attending St. Louis University, they suggested that instead of going to school, Don would have been better off going to work and doing whatever possible to help the family financially. While going to school, Don had given thought to asking out this young woman who happened to be a close friend of our cousin's family. They suggested to us the father would never agree or allow him to date his daughter.

This did nothing other than motivate my brother even further. Don would prove that only he alone was the captain of his ship. Your accomplishments and success in life are what determine your place in this world. He would go on to a remarkable career and financial success through hard work, strong efforts, deep commitment, and discipline. This far exceeded all his goals and expectations.

***

Mary Stephen's son, Art, had completed his junior college business education and took a job in the field of accounting. She could not have been prouder of her son. The job was out of town, which meant he would be leaving home. Her second son, Jimmy, took over Art's weekend job at our restaurant.

Our day waitress, Laverne, decided it was time for a change and announced she was moving on. It was becoming obvious that our afternoon dining room business was going down, and in all probability, that was the biggest motive behind her leaving our employment. Although she did not care too much for Dad, she learned to tolerate his ways and mannerisms. She enjoyed and relished her friendship with my mom, and it was the main reason behind her staying on for as long as she did.

I truly do not know what happened to our waitresses, Laverne and Bee, or where they landed jobs. It would not be surprising to me if they ended up back working for their old boss. The place where Phil Polizzi opened his new barbeque spot in Afton, Mo.

This created an opportunity for a new waitress or waiter to step in. Dad took little time replacing Laverne, and it was a real doozy of a choice. Val looked to be a man in his fifties, an ex-convict recently let out of prison for murdering his wife. He vehemently pleaded his innocence, swearing that he did not do it. This is not surprising since most people accused of a crime have always willingly confessed their innocence.

All I can say is that Val must have been quite convincing. It can be exceedingly difficult for an ex-convict to land any type of work. Dad may have felt compassion for this man who must have been desperately in search of a good-paying job. Even so, for the life of me, I cannot explain or understand what occurred weeks later.

It was summertime, and on certain weekdays, I would spend time at our restaurant. On this day, the St. Louis Cardinals were playing an afternoon game at home. In the spur of a moment, Dad walked over to me and asked, "How would you like to go to the ballgame this afternoon with…." I quickly began opening my mouth to eagerly respond "yes" before stopping in my tracks by what I heard next, "Val." Looking around, I noticed our waiter, Val, hanging out in the dining room section of the restaurant.

I wanted to give Dad the first degree on how or why this all came about. All he expected or wanted to hear from me was a yes or no answer, not twenty questions. It may have taken a little longer to answer his question than expected, but I gave the only possible answer. "Yes," I replied emphatically. The idea of saying "No" to seeing a Cardinal baseball game in person was not a part of my vocabulary. I had yet to get the chance to know our new waiter all that well. Undoubtedly, I felt a bit hesitant and a little uncomfortable going to the ball game with Val, but c'mon, it was the Cardinals!

Val and I began our walk down Sullivan Avenue. It was a three-block journey to Grand Avenue, and the stadium was on the other side of the street down a block. After we had gotten about halfway there, Val said to me, "We need to make a quick stop by my place. It is a couple of houses down the street here." At this point, I thought to myself, "Wait a minute, this was not part of the plan." Suddenly, I began to feel a little uncomfortable and nervous about my decision to go to this game.

As we entered the flat, a much older-looking couple appeared in the room, and Val introduced me to them. "These extremely nice and generous people have allowed me to rent out their spare bedroom," he explained. Val seemed profoundly grateful to this couple for taking him into their home. Taking only a moment to grab what he needed out of his room, we once again headed for the ballpark. I felt quite relieved after clearing that hurdle, and we made it to the game with no additional detours.

Val bought us tickets in the Pavilion section of the ballpark, which is one step above the bleacher tickets. The bleachers were situated in the center and left field parts of the ballpark and farthest away from home plate. There, you sat on benches with no back while at the same time exposed to the sun with no roof for cover. In the pavilion section, you were still sitting on benches with no back, but you were in the right field and a little closer to home plate. Also, there was a roof over your head, which made it a bit cooler than the bleachers, especially on a sunny day.

Val and I chatted off and on throughout the entire game, enjoying each other's company. He offered to buy me stuff like peanuts and soda, but I did not want him to spend any more of his money, so I politely refused. And to top it all off, the Cardinals won the game, which is what I cared about most. Val and I returned to the restaurant without a hitch. I have thought about the varied reasons why Dad may have allowed Val to take me to the ballgame. The one thing I felt certain about is he did this out of the kindness of his heart. And just maybe, it was more for Val than for me. He did not stay on the job with us much longer. I only hoped for his sake that leaving us led to a better opportunity and continued finding his way back into society.

***

After summer ended, our restaurant business began its struggle to keep up the current level of sales. There was always a drop in business after the summer, but Dad could see with his own two eyes the surrounding area and neighborhood continuing to change, and not for the better. He started considering the possibility of opening a second restaurant in a better location.

There happened to be a piece of property that had been available for quite a while that had caught Dad's interest. The place had formerly been known as Johnny's Out of Town. I recall that whenever we visited Giovanni's Italian grocery, we would go past Johnny's with their large parking lot filled with cars. However, the building had now been vacant for a considerable amount of time. That alone should have begged the question of why, for that matter, it had shut down.

Once again, my brother Don stepped in and attempted to advise our father to reconsider taking on this venture. He suggested, "Dad, if you want to look at another opportunity, maybe consider a successful brand name." I can still remember the suggestion about looking into a franchise and mentioning McDonald's. It was starting to get real momentum and good brand recognition around the country, and the franchise price was still very reasonable.

Dad scoffed at this idea, commenting, "Some little hamburger joint does not compare or can touch a decent restaurant and bar." If Dad could have only realized the potential of a McDonald's franchise, who knows what might have been? Of course, the financing might still have been an issue. However, this suggestion was another example and preview of my brother's investing genius and future success in the investment world over the next fifty-plus years.

Ignoring the opinions and suggestions from my eldest brother, Dad put the wheels into motion and set out on the path to becoming the owner of a second restaurant. First, he needed to find out what it was going to take to acquire Johnny's. The requirement was that he sign a one-year lease, and that was acceptable to him. Secondly, it would be necessary for him to get this new place up and running. This meant trusting and convincing someone whom he already had in mind to be agreeable and willing to take over the business reigns at Elliot & Sullivan.

The only logical and available choice in the family was my brother, Nick. At the time, he was already working two jobs and having fun going out on the town every weekend. These may have been reasons behind what led to him failing out of his first semester at college.

Dad was able to persuade my twenty-year-old brother to take on the responsibility of running our restaurant on Elliott & Sullivan. He was putting faith, hope, and trust into the prospect that Nick would be able to hold up the restaurant's current income level in the same way Dad had managed to do for almost three years. Looking back, it seems doubtful as to whether either one of them truly questioned the extremity of this task. In other words, take into consideration the amount of dedication and hard work asked and required of this young man. And, more importantly, whether this was even somehow attainable.

Mom continued to go over to Elliott & Sullivan in the mornings, and then Nick would come in and take over from early afternoon until close. Our waitress, Mary, went along with Dad to help with starting up the second restaurant. This meant a replacement needed to fill her shoes at Elliott & Sullivan. I have no idea who Dad ended up hiring to take over this key role. Nick suggested to me that Mary's replacement was this "Hoosier." This is a word referred to, in greater St. Louis, as a pejorative for an unintelligent or uncultured person. This scenario could very well have left our customers at Elliott & Sullivan with a different point of view and perspective. Giving the appearance of an evening business under new management handed over to a twenty-year-old young man and very possibly an inexperienced or incapable waitress.

There was no open fire pit for barbecue at Johnny's Out of Town. Dad believed offering barbecue ribs would be a good addition to the menu. So, twice a week, he drove over to Elliott & Sullivan, bringing back a sizable portion of cooked ribs over to the new place. He would also pull other products from the shelves whenever running short on certain items. These kinds of decisions and other moves did not help in leaving Elliott & Sullivan in the position to continue to succeed. Dad's commitment and focus locked onto the success of his new restaurant. He expected that Nick would do everything necessary to hold Vitale's Bar-B-Que together, keeping sales steady while he worked at getting this new place off the ground.

The first and biggest setback to our new spot occurred when we did not secure a full liquor license for the restaurant and bar. The cost might have been too high to figure into the budget, and the only affordable liquor license we could obtain was for beer. The other possibility may have been Dad's inability to secure a license due to his previous two jail sentences he served around 1940. In hindsight, the previous owners must have gotten a substantial portion of their profits from their bar business. The fact we could not sell any liquor products other than beer put our restaurant and bar business at a huge disadvantage.

Here was this formerly popular restaurant possessing a separate bar room and a big, beautiful bar. This bar was long enough to seat ten to twelve people easily and comfortably. Also, there were additional side tables for those who might want to choose to eat in this area. However, it would be void of any hard liquor-drinking crowd, thus losing substantial profits and potential customers.

Dad's thought process may have been that his other restaurant only offered beer, and it had done fine without the sale of hard liquor. What he might have failed to understand is this new restaurant was a completely different venue from his barbecue restaurant in the city. Johnny's Out of Town had been quite a popular spot due in part to the large bar area business it attracted. All this potential profit from the sale of hard liquor drinks and wine for the restaurant and bar was being incorrectly discounted. Dad's vision was too narrow, and his only intent was to make a go of this place off the food menu. I wonder, did the bar element that he dealt with in his young days at his father's tavern cause him to avoid the prospect of running a restaurant and bar?

He was running the kitchen with limited help due to budget restraints. Our waitress, Mary, would take orders and shout out the meal orders into the kitchen. This type of behavior may have been acceptable at Elliott & Sullivan, but this restaurant was a little more upscale than the barbecue joint in North St. Louis City. Unfortunately, such insight into these kinds of mistakes always occurs after the fact. Also, it would be difficult and unfair to find all faults limited to these mistakes. I am simply noting these pitfalls could well have influenced the potential failure of this business venture.

As for myself, I became caught up in the St. Louis Cardinals' unbelievable and remarkable pennant run. The 1964 Cardinals' comeback is the greatest of all time. They leapfrogged six teams to win the pennant after being ten games back with around one-third of the season to go. This was their first pennant in eighteen years and my first time witnessing one. Back then, televised baseball games during the season were of a limited number. So, I would envision every play through listening to the games over the city's popular radio station, KMOX-AM.

They would also go on to win the World Series over the New York Yankees in seven games. For the life of me, I could never understand the actions of Cardinal's manager, Johnny Keane, on the following day. Here was this man with an excellent opportunity to sign a huge long-term contract, and he chose to quit the team a day after they won the World Series. He then joined up with the Yankees as their manager. They fired him in his first mid-season with the team. The following winter, he passed away due to a fatal heart attack.

Other than washing the dishes or occasionally bussing a table, there was a limited number of things I could do to help at the new place. Dad finally got additional help in the kitchen, and Mary began doing what little she could to help in the kitchen. After leaving Elliott and Sullivan in the afternoon, Mom would show up at Johnny's to help with the early dinner crowd. Oh yes, and there was one other person that Dad recruited to the restaurant, my sister, Theresa. She had recently graduated from high school and had yet to find an acceptable job. Therefore, she drew the short straw and got the assignment to work at Johnny's.

Over the first few months, the restaurant's clientele began to grow slowly but surely. This place was a dining establishment and not set up for take-out food orders. Since there was no real bar business, most sales had to come from dining room service. There was no question that the inability to offer wine or hard liquor to dining guests was hurting growth and sales. However, at this point, there was no turning back.

Mom and Dad continued to believe and rely on their cooking and food preparation to grow their restaurant business.

The neighborhood area around our four-family flat, which Dad managed for Grandma, had deteriorated greatly. The property values in this section of North St. Louis were diminishing badly. The immediate area was moving toward the poverty line, and our collection of rent was almost non-existent. I am not even sure if there were tenants still living on the property. Besides that, Dad could no longer be available to watch over and take care of the property. There was no point in hanging onto it any further. We were extremely fortunate to unload it for a decent price.

Dad broke the news to Grandma and surrendered a small portion of the sale to her. She became terribly upset and cried for a couple of days. Once again, a feeling of economic betrayal crossed her mind, the same way it happened after her husband passed away. Mom did her best to explain the reasons and developments that made it necessary to sell. Grandma had gotten too old and did not understand such things; explanations were of no use to her, and it fell on deaf ears.

(The 5th Inning)

---1965---

Shortly after the Christmas and New Year holidays, our family began looking forward to the next wedding taking place in February 1965. My sister, Catherine, would be getting married after a long four-year courtship. Her fiancé, Dennis Maxwell, will tell you that God played a hand in her meeting him for the first time.

It all started at "The Circle" Steak n Shake. Dennis and two of his friends were making their way toward the downtown area of St. Louis. As their car maneuvered its way around the giant-sized roundabout, the driver took the turn too sharply and could only watch as his wallet above the sun visor flew out the car window. In going back to recover the wallet, they spotted two cute girls sitting in a car at the Steak n Shake parking lot. This happened to be my sister, Catherine, and her girlfriend, Rosemary. Without a moment's hesitation, Dennis proclaimed, "The redhead is mine," and fortunately for him, those words became true.

He was in awe of her beauty, and while talking to her, the thought crossed his mind, "This girl is too young for me." Dennis would not believe she was old enough to date until she produced a driver's permit that proved her legal age. With a feeling of great relief, he popped the all-important question, "Would you like to go out on a date with me?" Catherine knew better than to go out with a stranger. "My parents will not allow me to date anyone they don't know," she explained. This did not dissuade him from pursuing her. He then suggested, "What about if I come over some evening to meet your parents?" And so, he met with them and got their approval to date Catherine.

During his four years attending the University of Missouri, Dennis would come home from time to time to visit my sister. He came from a family where his parents got into big arguments and fights before their marriage finally ended in a divorce. Thoughts of marriage were the farthest thing from his mind. The problem was he could not get this girl out of his mind, although he tried extremely hard by taking out other girls at the university. Up till the day they were married, he continuously asked Catherine the same question. "Are you going to change who you are after we get married?" And she always gave him the same worn-out reply, "No, Dennis."

Our sister, Theresa, was happy and excited to be the maid of honor for her sister's wedding. About one week before the wedding, she was working in the kitchen of our second restaurant. When turning on the gas oven, she delayed lighting it, and the fire igniting from the oven promptly flared up. She received burns around her face, hair, and neck.

One of our two cousins, who were medical doctors, came over immediately that evening and applied a special salve to her face and neck. "The thick base of makeup saved your face and helped prevent you from getting a worse burn," he surmised. Later in the week, she went out in search of and found an acceptable wig that closely matched her hair color. Thus, my sister worked through this unfortunate mishap and was able to gracefully conduct her duties as the maid of honor.

For my sister Catherine's wedding, my younger sister, Maria, was the junior bridesmaid, and I was the junior groomsman. Immediately following the ceremony, we exited the church, and I prepared to do my part in the 'throwing of rice' tradition. As the wedding couple exits the church, tossing rice symbolizes a shower of fertility. According to the Sicilian wedding tradition, they use wheat instead of rice. The meaning is the same: a symbol of wealth and fertility. Since we had no wheat, rice would have to suffice.

I may have been overly excited and worked up, so I grabbed handfuls of rice and threw them as hard as I could right into the groom's face. Oh yes, I could be a real stinker during those days! In a wedding picture closeup taken inside the limousine shortly thereafter, you can see tiny red marks on my brother-in-law's face caused by the rice I launched at him.

My parents had gone through the same process and preparations for this wedding as they did with my first sister. Mom searched long and hard and found a perfect, large wedding hall for a very reasonable price. And once again, they managed all the catering services for over three hundred guests. When dinner was over, they got an opportunity to visit with their guests and enjoy the balance of the wedding. Although it took an exceptional amount of time, work, and effort, the happiness of this day, along with the look of joy on their daughter's face, made it all worthwhile.

The first three marriages were all conducted inside a Catholic Church. I thought it was a bit surprising that none of my in-laws were members of the Catholic faith. However, all three had become very observant of what our faith meant to us and how it reflected in the way our family showed each other care, love, and affection. By the time they were married or not long after, all three of them decided to join closer with their spouse and converted to the Catholic faith.

***

Spring was approaching, and the business at Elliott & Sullivan was continuing to decline in sales, month after month. The second restaurant was slowly growing and working its way toward being profitable. Mother's Day arrived, and we had the biggest day in our brief history at Johnny's, giving us a glimmer of hope. It became a short-lived optimism because Elliot & Sullivan kept continuing to decline, and the tremendous success of Mother's Day was looking more like an anomaly.

The year-long lease on Johnny's was getting closer to its end. At Elliott & Sullivan, there was this long-term commitment with more than six years to go. Weekly sales were continuing to plunge downward. This left Dad with no other alternative but to end his lease with the second restaurant and return to the first one. He vowed to restore his struggling business on Elliott and make the best of an exceedingly difficult and compromising situation.

Miraculously, within a matter of weeks after my father's return, we began seeing an upturn in customer activity and sales. As always, Mom continued working at the restaurant in the morning, and Dad would join her before the afternoon rush. Our waitress, Mary, also returned with us. She would come later in the day to relieve Mom, helping with the dinner crowd and late evening business. On Fridays, Mom would drive home to pick me up and take me to the restaurant. Then, she would stick around during the Friday evening rush before going back home. I stayed till closing and then returned on Saturdays and Sundays with Dad.

***

Every summer, there was a special place that I always looked forward to visiting. My stay with them would last for a week or two. It was my Uncle Steve's and Aunt Sara's home. This would always be the highlight of my summer. My cousin Donnie was one year older than me, and my cousin Nicky was one year younger than me. We very much enjoyed each other's company and got along great together. I cannot remember ever having one fight or argument with them in all the years and times we spent together.

Whenever the three of us were together, especially playing ball, it was my best of times. They were both excellent athletes and extremely competitive, which made it even more fun. In the morning, shortly after breakfast, the three of us would head out and gather up other neighborhood boys to join us in playing one of three games: Wiffle ball, Indian ball, or street Football. We would spend the best part of every daylight hour outside playing all those different games, and by God, I loved it. It was my once-a-year opportunity to play sports all day long with my close cousins and other friends.

Indian ball is a sport that originated in the late 1940s in St. Louis, Missouri. The area of play can be any size, from a regular field to a side yard or street. We could play the game with anywhere from four to ten players. There are three separate ways in which a ball goes into play. The way we played the game was when the batter tossed the ball in the air, and he would hit it himself. There are infielders and outfielders to make plays on the ball. Any ball hit in the air or on the ground with no error meant you were out. If it got by the infielders or not fielded cleanly, it was a single. If it got by the outfielders, it was a double, and if it went over an outfielder's head on the fly, it was a home run.

The only football we played was on the street where my cousins lived. On every football play called, we would consider every corner and line separating each concrete block on the street. After setting up each play, we carefully checked and made sure the street was clear of oncoming traffic before running the play. We stopped after each play to set up the next one and once again checked for traffic before running the play.

However, it was the wiffle ball games that ended up taking the main stage and becoming our favorite game to play. We played all these games in my cousin's backyard. The fascination with this game had to do with the fine art of pitching and hitting. The pitching was all about the amount of speed and curve placed on the ball. Proper execution of this by the pitcher made the flight of the ball very deceptive, and it was difficult to make good contact. This required you to achieve a proper swing reaction based on the amount of speed and curve placed on the ball. Hitting a ball into fair territory was a rewarding accomplishment. Usually, these games would be close, knock-down, drag-out battles, and quite often, they ended in arguments between my two cousins, Nicky and Donnie.

In the early years, the younger of the two, Nicky, would always get upset at one point in the game. It would usually occur during a pivotal call or point in the game that might determine the winner. If he could not win the argument against his older brother, Nicky would run inside the house and start complaining to my Aunt Sara. He would tell her that Donnie was either cheating or not playing fair.

Nicky would return within minutes and announce to his older brother, "Mommie wants you." It seemed like this same scenario played out every time they got into an argument over a game. The two of them were the best two players of all the kids playing, and it always seemed a necessity for them to be on separate teams. This was the main reason behind all this arguing. One summer, it got so bad that Aunt Sara decided they could only play if they were on the same team. Fortunately, this ended up being a short-lived experiment because the teams became too one-sided.

We always stayed outside until the day reached darkness. In the summertime, that would sometimes be as late as 9 p.m. Uncle Steve liked his quiet alone time at night, so all of us kids had to be in bed with lights out around 10 p.m. Obviously, lights out did not mean sleep at least not to our way of thinking. In one corner, Nicky and I slept in bunk beds, with me on the lower. Donnie slept in a twin bed in the corner directly to the left of us. In later years, they added another twin bed in the other corner for one of the younger brothers, Stevie.

All of us lay there in the dark at night talking, and sometimes we got to laughing a little too loud. The moment things started getting out of hand, we would hear footsteps coming from down the hallway. We would immediately get quiet just before the bedroom door opened. In these instances, nothing happened because we knew to at least pretend to be fast asleep. This would usually occur three or four times every night before we finally passed out from our long day of playing ball.

I remember being asleep early one morning and recovering from the previous day's sports activities. Then, I was shockingly awakened by blood-curdling screams coming directly from the floorboard below me. Hearing this person screaming and experiencing this kind of pain left me with the after-effects of a fearful, nagging, and irritating phobia. Once this disturbance subsided, I got out of bed to investigate what could have caused such a horrific outburst. It just so happened that my cousin, Nicky, had gotten up early that morning and was outside playing when a bee stung him right in the head.

Over the next twenty-five years or so, I did everything possible to try and mask my phobia and fear. Whenever I spotted a bee, I would try to unsuspectingly flee the area if it got too close to me. At the same time, I would raise my hands in the air, being wary of protecting my head. I had become obsessively frightened by the prospect of a bee stinging me in the head.

The phobia did not subside until after my parents retired. Dad was sitting on his riding mower cutting the lawn on his three-acre property. He unknowingly rode over a nest of wasps who took revenge by swarming around him and stinging him over a dozen times in his belly and chest. He finally got away by making a mad dash into the house. I knew that Dad was tough. However, seeing him recover from that kind of attack and the number of stings pushed me into a different state of mind. If he could go through an attack and suffer through all those stings, then I was being ridiculous, overly excited, and obsessed over the prospect of one bee sting.

It was always a sad time for me whenever vacation time at my cousin's house ended, but then I knew and took comfort in the thought of going home to my own wonderful family.

***

After making his return to Elliott & Sullivan, Dad allowed me to begin taking on additional duties at the restaurant. One thing I started doing was to answer the phone and take down carry-out food orders. I also bagged the carry-out orders and, in time, would begin helping fill out the orders. Another thing I did was set up sandwich orders by placing onions and pickles on the plate. I filled cups with coleslaw and potato salad for dinner plate orders. Then, cut two pieces of bread in half, diagonally, and put half of each side with the slaw or potato salad cup in the middle.

Before I knew it, Dad began telling me to start putting hamburgers on the grill, flip them over, and lay down buns on the grill for toasting. Other times, he would tell me to keep watch over the fryer. He explained to me when food in the fryer came floating to the top of the oil, it was fully cooked. I would then raise the basket up and out of the oil and give it a good shake before hanging it onto the lip of the fryer, allowing the remaining oil to drip off.

I finally got an opportunity to make pizza. It was the one cool thing I had been waiting for so long to do. This process was quite simple to learn. Our pizza shells came prefabricated; in other words, already made. The next step was to ladle the pizza sauce evenly about and around the entire pizza shell. I then sprinkled garlic powder over the pizza sauce and added any additional desired toppings. These included pepperoni, sausage, hamburger, mushroom, green peppers, onions, and anchovies, all of which were already prepared and pre-cut. All I had to do was add the toppings onto the pizza shell. Nowadays, all kinds of meats, vegetables, and fruit have become additional toppings on pizza.

Lastly, we added our cheese to the pizza shell. Although there are various kinds of cheeses used on a pizza, our topping of choice was mozzarella. I would grab a handful of shredded mozzarella cheese and evenly spread it around the entire pizza. It was always a clever idea to cup my hand along the edge of the pizza shell while distributing the cheese to keep it from spilling over the edge. Then, topped it off with a dash of oregano seasoning, and it was ready for the oven.

Mary Stephen's second son, Jimmy, had left our employment and took a full-time job. With him out of the picture, it gave me the opportunity to experience pizza making on the weekends. Our restaurant business continued to pick up even further with Dad and his waitress, Mary, back in place. There was just one problem: Dad could prepare pizzas for the oven within five minutes, but it took me closer to ten minutes. One night, it was getting extremely busy, and he came over to check on how I was coming along with the pizza orders. Abruptly pushing me aside, he took over and remarked in his specific, critical manner, "You're making pizza, not painting a picture."

Around one year after Dad took over the restaurant from Phil Polizzi, it was necessary to slightly raise prices on barbecue items; later, he had to raise prices on other items. Although the timing was not the best, once again, Dad felt another increase was necessary to keep up with the cost of overall business overhead expenses. The price of dinners now ranged from $1.25 to $1.75. This created a total sales boost of around twenty percent. Despite all the price increases, our restaurant continued its slow resurgence from the previous year's lows. Weekly sales continued to creep back up to the amount they were before leaving Elliot & Sullivan to run the failed attempt of a second restaurant.

The overall business was still down around twenty percent in comparison to our first few years in business. It was the menu price increases and Sunday openings that allowed us to achieve the sales level of our first two years. Without question, the catalyst behind our diminishing business continued to be the changing demographics within the neighborhood.

One other problem was that white families were fleeing to both the north and south county areas. The loyal customers moving to the north were returning, but it would usually be for take-out orders. However, customers moving to the south side were more likely to visit Phil's new barbecue joint because it was closer to them. Also, they felt more comfortable traveling to that section of town.

Being that it was summertime, I began spending more time at the restaurant. Sometimes, I would go in early on weekdays with Mom and do whatever possible to help get things ready for opening. We would leave the restaurant around midafternoon and begin making our way home.

It was there, and then I discovered one thing mom did out of necessity but particularly loved doing. To stop by and shop at this quaint little clothing store on Grand Avenue. It offered clothing for men, women, and children. Mom roamed around the entire place, looking over clothing items and searching for anything cut down in price. She would then determine if a piece of clothing appealed to her and seemed appropriate or purposeful for either herself or one of the younger children in our family. She knew all the salespeople inside that store and constantly worked them over to get the price knocked down even further.

Of course, Mom had no choice but to do this with everything she purchased apart from gasoline for the car and certain grocery items. If she had not done this throughout all those years, it would never have been possible to adequately meet her living standards and to fulfill the demands of properly caring for her home and family.

It was incredibly boring for me to stick around watching this entire process inside the clothing store. Sometimes, to get me out of her hair, Mom allowed me to walk next door to Woolworths 5 & 10. This was a former American chain of general-merchandise retail stores and based on the original concept of these stores (i.e., a store that sells all items in stock for ten cents or less).

I would browse around and check out all the cheap toy items priced for as little as a dime. Every so often, I had enough money to buy a paper kite and would fly it until a tree or roof eventually snatched it away. Other times, I purchased one of these thin-pressed wooden airplanes with little red plastic propellors and wheels. Once put together, the next thing to do is wind up the propeller, attached to a long rubber band stretching across the bottom of the plane. Then I laid the plane and its wheels on a hard street surface. Holding onto the fragile plane and its propeller, I carefully let go of them simultaneously and watched it take off, flying.

Another item available for purchase for the price of one dime was a foam rubber ball around the size of a baseball. I enjoyed bouncing or throwing it off the walls outside of the restaurant and my home. Sometimes, I just threw it in the air as high as possible and tried catching it coming down. Undoubtedly, I must have this great obsession with watching things moving through the air.

***

Since our restaurant was not open on Mondays, and it was summertime, I took the opportunity to ride along with Dad. He would run errands and do things he could not accomplish on other days of the week. First, we stopped at the various companies with whom we purchased wholesale foods for our restaurant. While there, Dad would take a little time to chat with the proprietors before placing a new order and paying off the previous bill.

St. Louis had this one exceptionally large produce market aptly called "Produce Row." It would be our next stop of the day. This landmark spot also played a part in a Hollywood movie. "The Hoodlum Priest" was partially filmed in the St. Louis area back in 1961. It is a true story about Father Charles Clark, a minister to street gangs. Produce Row included this extremely wide quarter-of-a-mile-long parking lot for all incoming/outgoing eighteen-wheelers and other trucks and vehicles. On each side of this long block, you would see rows and rows of enormous concrete storage facilities with a loading dock to accommodate the eighteen-wheelers. Above each of these large units, painted in huge letters, were the names of the property owners. All these units varied by the produce they carried or currently had in stock.

These eighteen-wheelers would come in and unload the produce into the merchant's storage facility. All other trucks and vehicles came in to pick up their produce orders from a chosen merchant's storage facility. There were certain merchants that Dad favored over others. We would stop and check with them first to see whether they had what we needed for the restaurant. Also, my family enjoyed all varieties of fruits, and without fail, he would look around for a bushel, box, or crate of any fruit in stock selling for a good discount price. He was always on the lookout for our favorites: peaches, plums, apricots, cherries, grapes, strawberries, and watermelons.

Sometimes, I would get lucky and manage to convince Dad to stop at this music store in the downtown area. I walked around the entire place and would look for current hit songs to replace the records, getting no play on the jukebox. Dad would usually pick one song by one of his favorite Italian-American artists. Then, he would allow me to pick four or five other records. I always wondered, did he let me choose these records to be nice, or was it because of my persuasive suggestion that I knew better about the more popular songs of the day?

After running all the errands, we would head over to the restaurant. Once there, we began doing, by far, the newest and worst duty ever assigned to me. Every Monday, it became a necessity to vigorously swab down and clean all the floors. Due to the time constraints, Dad could only mop these floors thoroughly once a week.

It was a nasty job, but somebody had to do it. Dad certainly had no intention of paying someone else to do it, so the duty fell on him and whomever he could get to help, in other words, me. The cleaning areas included the main dining room, the front section, the back dining cove, restrooms, the entire kitchen, and the storage room.

First, we started with a good soaking of the floors using a strong soap detergent with vinegar added to the mix. The smell was extraordinarily strong. We soaped down all the stiff rubber slats inside the kitchen, then dragged them into the backyard, hosed them down, and left them out to dry. Next, we soaped down all the floors, one by one. Then, we took buckets of fresh water and cleaned up all the soaped-down floors. Next, we dry-mopped all the floors, picking up any excess water. The complete process was a long, arduous task that took us at least two hours.

I suppose it was not too bad until the school year started. On Mondays, after getting home from school and having dinner, I waited for the dreaded announcement. Dad would inform me it was time to make our way to the restaurant and clean the floors. We returned home just in time for me to get in bed. This became a weekly ordeal and eventually caused me to abhor this awful task. The only good thing about it was I did not worry about doing my homework on those nights. And who is to say I would have done it anyway?

***

For years, during the summertime, my cousins Donnie and Nicky would take turns visiting my home for one week. This summer, it was my cousin Nicky's turn to spend the week. It just so happened the Los Angeles Dodgers were in town that weekend to play three games against the St. Louis Cardinals. Sandy Koufax, now at the height of his illustrious career, was pitching against the Cardinals on Sunday afternoon. There was nothing Nicky and I wanted more than to see Koufax pitch with lofty expectations of our hometown team beating this great pitcher.

I can still remember Dad calling my older brother Mariano to his side. He handed over three dollars, instructing him to take my cousin and me to this Cardinals-Dodgers ballgame. Then I overheard my brother say, "Dad, you know this is barely enough money to get us into the bleachers," I then heard him respond to my brother. "That's okay, just do it."

I could not care less if it was the bleachers. Would I rather have been closer? Sure, why not? All that mattered to me was being able to watch Sandy Koufax pitch a game in person against our St. Louis Cardinals. I do not believe we had a drink or anything to eat. Once again, it did not matter. My complete focus was strictly on the game and watching this future Hall of Fame legend pitch his game.

Then, I heard my brother, simply out of curiosity, ask my cousin Nicky, "Where do you normally sit when your dad takes you to a Cardinal ballgame?" I watched as Nicky pointed to the opposite side of the field behind home plate. Admittedly, I did for a moment feel a little sad, but I tried hard not to dwell on the fact we could only afford the bleachers.

Sandy Koufax performed another one of his pitching gems, striking out eleven batters and going the entire nine-inning game. The Cardinals only scored one run until the bottom of the ninth inning when Curt Flood got on base, and Ken Boyer knocked him in, making the score 4-2 with a runner on base. For a moment, the entire crowd got a bit excited as the tying run stepped into the batter's box. However, the great Koufax ended that threat right then and there. It was still a wonderful game and a day to remember, and the spot from where we watched the game seemed completely irrelevant to Nicky and me.

***

As the summer was ending, Mom received a phone call from our parish school. They informed her that my youngest brother, Rio, would not be admitted into the first grade at St. Casimir's. The incoming first-grade class was full, and the school board had to make tough decisions. My parents were not donating enough funds to the weekly church contribution envelopes. Other parishioners wishing for their children to attend St. Casimir's first-grade class were making their expected financial contributions.

Disheartened by this decision, Mom reached out directly to our pastor to plead her case. I am certain the pastor apologized for the decision they had to make. However, he did not have any desire to take responsibility or show any interest in going to the school board and trying to appeal their decision.

As far as my sister and I, we had no idea as to what our fate was going to be regarding acceptance into St. Casimir the next school year. Mom was very hurt and a bit enraged over the purpose and reasoning behind their decision to deny her last child attendance at the parish school. Times were changing, and more than ever, money talked. She allowed frustration and anger to get the best of her as she proclaimed to our pastor, "When I see you standing up at the altar, I will no longer be seeing my pastor; instead, I will be seeing a big dollar sign over your head."

These circumstances and the situation it put us in did not sit well with Mom. She quickly began taking steps to rectify the matter. Every single one of her children had attended and gone through the Catholic grade school system, and she was not about to let this change with her youngest child.

St Augustine's parish and school were only three blocks away from our restaurant. My youngest brother got permission to attend their parish school's first-grade classroom. I do not know what she said or how she did it, but Mom figured out a way to get him into that school. It might have had something to do with our restaurant being located inside the parish neighborhood.

After the school year began, Rio would travel once again with Mom to the restaurant every weekday morning. After dropping him off at the school, she made her way over to the restaurant. She worked and stayed there until it was time to pick my brother up from school. Then, she would return home to fulfill her household duties for the remainder of the day.

Gratefully, Maria and I were able to return to St. Casimir School for the upcoming year. Pope Pius XII named Saint Casimir the special patron of all youths, and it seemed cool to me that his name was on my Catholic grade school. I would be entering the seventh grade. Upon reaching my classroom that first day of school, I found myself pleasantly surprised. For the very first time, my classroom teacher was going to be a man. Mr. Fuchs was a noticeably young man and, in all probability, a recent college graduate. Although I was only in his classroom for one semester, he turned out to be quite a personable instructor. His way of teaching made our classroom more fun and entertaining. There were a couple of things he revealed to us that stood out to me to this very day.

Mr. Fuchs allowed our classroom to know something a bit out of the ordinary regarding one of his close relatives. Thinking back, I cannot recall his distinct family relationship with this man. His name was Klaus Fuchs, a German theoretical physicist and atomic spy. He supplied information from the American, British, and Canadian Manhattan Project to the Soviet Union during and shortly after World War II. While at the Los Alamos National Laboratory, Fuchs was responsible for significant theoretical calculations relating to the first nuclear weapons and, later, early models of the hydrogen bomb. After his conviction in 1950, he served nine years in prison in the United Kingdom, then migrated to East Germany, where he resumed his career as a physicist and scientific leader.

I never understood Mr. Fuchs's intent to inform us of these details. Besides that, I was unable to determine whether he was confessing or bragging. Either way, it did not seem to be something a person would particularly want to claim, share, or admit.

The other thing was his so-called "Class Ladder" designation for all people of this world. He went into specific details explaining all three classes and the three levels in each class for a total of nine levels. He began with the upper-class levels. These were the upper-upper, upper-middle, and upper-lower classes.

The three upper classes were not based on any level of professionalism; they had to do solely with your last name. For instance, Rothschild or Rockefeller would be upper-upper class. Ford or Kennedy was upper-middle class. He then mentioned other well-known family names that fell into the upper-lower class.

He then went into the three middle-class levels. The middle-upper, middle-middle, and middle-lower classes were based on a combination of an individual's professional status level and net worth. For example, the middle-upper level would be your well-known professional actor, athlete, artist, upper-level businessman, or CEO. The middle-middle level was most likely doctors, lawyers, engineers, professors, scientists, and a variety of business professionals, such as CPAs. The middle-lower would consist of people in well-paying positions who did not reach the level of professionalism found in the middle-middle class.

He concluded with a discussion of the three lower classes. The upper-lower, middle-lower, and lower-lower. These three classes were for individuals above the poverty line, around the poverty line, and below the poverty line.

After taking this all in, there seemed little doubt in my mind that, to a degree, these class levels do exist. Unfortunately, while they exist, they will continue to prey and feed on humanity's worst behavioral traits: greed, power, control, dishonesty, deception, and selfishness.

Shortly after the school year began, my parents decided to put our house on the market for sale. I do not know how much, if any, the problem with the parish school played in us moving. The other thing I did not know was the financial hardship we might have incurred from the opening and failure of our second restaurant. The loss of income from Elliot & Sullivan during that time most certainly contributed to our family's financial woes.

My older brother Mariano was still living at home and had recently taken charge of the family's finances. In so doing, he quickly came to the realization it would no longer be adding a portion of his income. Instead, he would be contributing to all of it to keep a roof over our heads.

In the years to come, Mariano chose to return to school part-time and eventually graduated from St. Louis University's night school program. During his younger days, and upon entering the seminary that first semester, his mind was not yet mature enough to meet or pass their academic standards. Although it might well have been the life chosen for himself, due to our family's history of late bloomers, his early years left him unable to pass his studies and have this come to fruition.

I think my brother may have decided that if he could not become devoted and married to the church, then his devotion would be to our family, who needed him. Mariano made it his job and duty to look after his immediate family. Although he financially helped support the family for years to come, he meant much more than that to us younger children. There is nothing this man would not do for us, and vice versa. He became our companion, friend, listener, teacher, and adviser. In short, Mariano was there in whatever way we needed him. Due in part to his devotion to our family, he did not make the time or find the opportunity for a love of his own. Therefore, he ended up staying single his entire life, making us his one and only family.

(The 6th Inning)

---1966---

Our house sold before the start of the new year, and shortly thereafter, we had to move into temporary housing. The contractor building our new home promised us a completion date before summer's end. This still left the problem of where my sister Maria and I would be going to school while in temporary housing. Once again, St Augustine's parish came to our rescue. My mother went to them a second time, and they permitted my sister and me to attend our second semester at their parish school.

There are good reasons to indicate this was the worst and most memorable semester for all four of us children still attending school. Early in the morning, we would pile into Mom's car. Our first stop was to drop off Lucia at her high school. We would then make our long drive into the city. Once there, Mom would drop Maria, Rio, and me off at St. Augustine's parish school before heading to work at the restaurant. After school, all three of us walked over to the restaurant.

Before going home, we had to make other stops. Lucia did not have any transportation to get from her high school to our current housing. So, every day, she rode the school bus to her girlfriend's home. She would stay at this girl's home until we came to pick her up. Besides that, Mom always wanted to drive by and check out the building progress at our new home site. All I wanted to do was go home and raise a fit because she had to check on it every day.

Our grandmother was in the late stages of cancer. Our two oldest brothers, Don and Mariano, served in the army reserves instead of waiting for the army draft. However, our brother Nick did not choose this path, and the army drafted him into service. The United States had been rapidly increasing its military presence in South Vietnam, and we all feared this could very well end up being our brother's destination.

Fortunately, Nick managed to avoid that awful war, and the army deployed him to the Demilitarized Zone (DMZ) in South Korea. The United States has a considerable number of army bases in this area. It is a strip of land running across the Korean Peninsula's thirty-eighth parallel north. The DMZ incorporates territory on both sides of the cease-fire line as it existed at the end of the Korean War (1950-1953). It is a border barrier established to serve as a buffer zone between North and South Korea.

Although he managed to avoid going to Vietnam, Nick would not escape the tragedies of war. After completing his term of service, they diagnosed him shortly thereafter with Multiple Sclerosis. There is no evidence of this disease existing in our family's history. Unfortunately, it does have a direct correlation to service members in the U.S. military who served on active duty overseas. Throughout the years, this horrible disease has slowly diminished my brother's health. Through all of it, he has managed this with ultimate grace, style, and a smile on his face.

After considering what our grandmother and brother Nick were facing, my plight in this so-called worst school semester ever seemed insignificant.

Undoubtedly, I was the culprit and my own worst enemy in causing this semester to be worse than expected. I had finally reached my teen years, and certain hormones must have been at play when I entered my new classroom for the first time. While taking a survey of everyone in the classroom, I was immediately smitten by this one girl.

For her age, Cathy Sanders was a very tall, well-endowed, and nicely put-together young girl with gorgeous chestnut-colored hair. I do not recall the color of her eyes, but they were quite stunning. I found myself with this desire to be around her, but not necessarily in a sexual way. My hormones had not yet completely kicked in or fully developed into those specific types of feelings.

The question became, what am I going to do about it? For that matter, was there anything that I could do about these feelings? I did not live in the neighborhood, and she did not sit anywhere near me in the classroom. This made it difficult to consider any kind of friendship. The next thought was to try and figure out a way to get her attention to notice me.

The class clown is a mischievous or impudent student who frequently disrupts the class with pranks or wry comments as a means of drawing attention to themselves. I quickly discovered that we already had two of these in the classroom. Happily and willingly, I found myself becoming the third musketeer in this group.

Tony and Marcus were the names of the other two class clowns or boys. I hit it off with them immediately. The way I saw it, there was a purpose behind them acting out in this manner. They were academically weak students. By performing in this way, they could hide or avoid that fact and save face. Our classroom teacher was a nun from the parish church. Sister Lawrence did not appreciate our continuous interruptions or the out-of-turn comments and remarks.

The Batman television series was extremely popular at the time. His sidekick, Robin, the Boy Wonder, used the phrase Holy (fill in the blank) an average of three times in every episode. Every so often, a certain subject or word would come up in the classroom, for example, matrimony. One or all three of us would then shout, "Holy Matrimony!" We worked in a tandem of outbursts, "Holy this, Holy that, Batman." This was one of the unusual ways we would disrupt our class and annoy Sister Lawrence.

Her method for putting a stop to these outbursts was by assigning us after-school punishment. Each day, after committing a classroom offense, she signed your name on the chalkboard for everyone to see. For every additional offense after that, an X would appear next to your name.

At the end of the day, for every X marked next to your name, the punishment was to write down twenty-five words and their definition using the dictionary. Without fail, the three of us would attain a sizable number of X marks by the end of the day. We rarely completed these punishment assignments because it would have taken all evening. Fortunately, Sister Lawrence had other duties, but she kept us in the classroom for as long as possible. At times, she forced us to stay after class for over an hour. This was quickly becoming a real problem for me. Mom had started to get upset and concerned about my continuous late arrivals to the restaurant after school.

****

Along with the new year came my dad's itch to get another dog. Part of his reasoning or excuse was to give our other dog, Rags, a little companionship. His interest and choice were leaning toward the purchase of a full-bred German Shepard or another term used in those days – a police dog.

These dogs are among the most intelligent in the world. They are easy to train, highly loyal, trustworthy, powerful, and formidable animals, calm under pressure, and not overly aggressive. I do not know why Dad chose the name Vickie, but she certainly matched the behavior traits of her breed.

Both of our dogs, Rags and Vickie, were females. Within months after Vickie came to our backyard, Dad began his search for a male dog. And this time, it would be an even bigger dog. Since the choice of a Great Dane did not work out so well, he decided to go in a different direction. This time, he was not going to mess around with any puppy. He brought into the yard a fully grown Giant Alaskan Malamute, an enormous dog that weighs anywhere from 100 to 200 pounds. Historically, their breeding allowed them to pull heavy goods between cities throughout Alaska. These dogs have been known to pull loads up to 1100 pounds. They have a very thick, medium-length coat to keep them warm in cooler climates. In addition, they are clever, playful, loyal, and can be quite territorial. For this one dog, the last trait noted, territorial, was the behavior that stood well above all others.

Aptly named Timber, it was to be a warning for all other dogs around him. This animal resembled the height of a Shetland pony and weighed over 150 pounds. As far as his behavior around other people, he was as gentle and kind a dog as you would be happy to own. However, this was not the case when it came to other dogs around him. At times, he would chase off our other two dogs, Vickie and Rags, especially if they moved toward any of the food or water bowls.

Timber would constantly receive a strong whack in the rear because he did not want the other dogs eating or drinking. Dad would sometimes become infuriated with this dog's behavior. One time, I saw him make a tight fist and pop this dog right in the head. Timber did not budge and just looked at him as though the punch had no effect.

Every day, Timber ate from an exceptionally large and wide bucket of food. Dad would first pour in dog food and then add a large amount of food scraps, which included a bunch of leftover rib bones. He would gobble up the entire bucket, inhaling a substantial amount of food at one time.

One day, I was standing in the backyard and watching Timber eating away at this monstrous bucket of food scraps. Suddenly, I noticed that he was attempting to hack something up. Within seconds, it became obvious the dog was in great distress, so I ran inside and yelled for Dad to come quickly.

He rushed into the yard and quickly observed the dog choking. Grabbing hold of Timber's mouth with his two bare hands, Dad pried open this huge animal's mouth as wide as possible. In the very back, lodged near his jaw inside the roof of his mouth, we spotted a rib bone lodged into his upper jawbone. The rib bone resembled that of a bridge going straight across the roof of his mouth.

Dad figured that he needed to produce a quick solution to save this dog. Shoving his entire hand down into Timber's mouth, he somehow managed to get his middle finger between the roof of the dog's mouth and the rib bone. He then pushed his finger downward, breaking the bone in half and relieving our dog from choking. I was not sure what kind of person would be willing to do something like that, but if nothing else, it made me realize that nothing he did should have surprised me.

Mom finally had enough of my walking into the restaurant after school and coming in late every day. At times, Sister Lawrence kept me after school extremely late. On those afternoons, I would find our car parked outside, and Mom would be waiting there with my younger sister and brother. After weeks of this nonsense, she realized it was time to have a meeting with Sister Lawrence.

The car ride home after their meeting became a very unpleasant one for me. Mom was visibly upset and extremely disappointed in me. She relayed to me how Sister Lawrence exposed me as this very disruptive force in her classroom. The sister accused me of inciting the other two boys, Marcus and Tony, to act up in class more than ever. Sister Lawrence then laid it on even thicker, and this hurt Mom more than me. "I thought a nice young Catholic boy coming from the county was going to be a wonderful influence on my students, not some destructive and disruptive force." She finished it off by informing Mom, "Your son does not turn in all of his assigned homework."

Going to school the next day, I tried my absolute best to mend my ways, but it was like asking an addict to stop drinking or smoking. Tony and Marcus continued their antics, and it was exceedingly difficult at times to keep from joining in on the fun. As this day ended, the worst event was yet to come. The door to our classroom opened, and my petite younger sister, Maria, came walking into the classroom with a somber and stoic look on her face.

She paraded up to Sister Lawrence's desk and announced, "I am here to pick up my brother's homework assignments." Without question, this received the biggest laugh of the day from my classmates. I sat there frozen at my desk, overwhelmed with embarrassment. This practice of my sister coming into the classroom to pick up my homework assignments every day went on for weeks till the end of the semester.

Due to my antics of having to stay after school every day, I happened to miss one of my dad's true acts of kindness. I had previously witnessed his acts of kindness for myself. For example, whenever law enforcement came into our place, he would charge them around half price for their meals. Every Saturday night, when the Salvation Army soldier came by, Dad would give them a donation and then accept their little weekend magazine.

My sister, Maria, never really got an opportunity to spend time at the restaurant, except for this brief time after school this one semester. She recounted to me a special act of kindness that occurred one afternoon. A family of four came wandering into the restaurant. As my sister watched them enter, she likened it to the plight of families during the Dust Bowl described by John Steinbeck in his novel "The Grapes of Wrath." They had an old pickup truck with all their belongings piled in the truck bed. She was unclear about the conversation the man was having with our dad, but it sounded like they had just arrived in town.

"I can offer you something to eat, but I don't have any work for you," said Dad. He then took the four of them to one of the tables and served them sandwiches and something to drink. The whole family ate very heartily and with great gusto and thoroughly enjoyed their meal. Afterward, Maria spotted our dad handing over dollar bills to the man. Dad may not have always seemed, to my sister, as some kind of hero, but she now witnessed him acting with compassion, kindness, and humanity toward his fellow man.

***

After school on Fridays, rather than go home, I chose to stay and help at the restaurant. St. Louis Cardinals' night games started around 8 p.m. On this night, April 22, 1966, the Friday dinner rush was coming to its end. The baseball season was only a week old, and the St. Louis Cardinals were only going to be playing a handful of games at the old stadium on Grand Avenue. After their first ten home games, they would be moving to their new stadium in the downtown area.

They first broke ground on the new stadium in May 1964. Cardinal baseball ownership had foreseen, just like Phil Polizzi, the economic downturn coming into the area neighborhoods. It was time to get out and move into a more favorable location. I desperately wanted to see one more ballgame before they moved downtown. Dad was generous enough to give me the money and permission to go to the game.

I feared and dreaded walking through the dark shadows down those three blocks over to Grand Avenue. The streets were not very well-lit, and this neighborhood was no longer the best place to be walking at night. Besides that, more Black people were continuing to move into the area. I developed a fear with an attitude that I needed to be wary and careful around them. I had concerns that, given the chance, there were certain Black people who might attempt or try to harm me.

To my way of thinking, there were good reasons for me to feel this way. Otherwise, why would people always be

136

moving to get away from them? Most white people would not dine in a place alongside them. I saw Black people dressed very poorly and sloppily. Even the various media platforms, movies, television, and the local news did not portray them in the best light. Naturally, I had become very suspicious and held to the belief that there must be something bad or wrong with a portion of these people.

However, I willingly accepted this risk, knowing it meant going to see a St. Louis Cardinals baseball game. Walking there from the restaurant, I arrived at the ballpark unscathed. I purchased a ticket to the general admission grandstand section. Once again, I had upgraded my seating away from the bleachers and pavilion sections of the ballpark. General admission seating was high above the playing field, stretching from the right-field corner to behind home plate and down into the left-field corner.

I looked up into the large grandstand area of the ballpark and calculated which of the remaining vacant seats offered me the best view. Finding a spot high above the area of third base, I sat down with a feeling of satisfaction in my choice of seats. As I began previewing the area and checking out my field of vision, I happened to look down at the row directly below me and one seat to the left.

I quickly identified the person sitting below me and felt stunned while overjoyed by this surprising outcome. Sitting there was none other than my cousin, Donnie, with whom I had spent so many great times over the past summers. I cannot imagine the odds of something like this happening. He was at the game with other boys from his Khoury League baseball team and their parents. Donnie was quite surprised himself, even more so once he realized I was attending the game all by myself.

We ended up having a wonderful time sitting together and watching the game. Donnie and I caught up on what was happening in our lives and reminisced about our past experiences together. I gave thought to those days when it would rain, sometimes all day. Donnie and Nicky would start pulling out all the board games, but we spent a good part of our time playing the All-Star baseball game.

This board game first appeared in 1941, and a special version of the game sells to this day. Only players who had performed in the major league all-star games could be in this board game. Each of the players' factual baseball statistics went strategically into one of eight categories and was printed on a circular card. The size of each category was determined by the players' factual statistics. The categories included walks, strikeouts, singles, doubles, triples, home runs, fly balls, and ground balls. Every card had a total of sixteen different sections: two sections for strikeouts, two for walks, two for singles, three for ground balls, four for fly balls, and one section for doubles, triples, and home runs.

The baseball player's statistical card went on a spinner, and the person whose team was at bat flicked the spinner positioned over the player's statistical card. The spinner came to rest on one of the sixteen sections, and this revealed the results of his at-bat performance. If the result was either a ground ball, fly ball, or a single, then the fielding outcome was determined by using a second spinner with fielding zones. The person whose team was in the field used a second spinner to determine the overall outcome of the fielding play.

Special plays, such as attempted steals, required the use of two special pink situation cards to indicate the result of those plays. The game did an excellent job of simulating the batter's performance and fielding plays, but it did not attempt to model the performance for individual pitchers. However, this did nothing to impede our excitement or enjoyment in playing the game.

My cousins had collected a wide range of Hall of Famer's cards from every era in baseball. We would sometimes mix and match players from different eras in our attempt to create various game scenarios. Once the game started, my cousin Donnie enjoyed playing the role of announcer and acted out play-by-play on every spin of the wheel. For me, this enhanced the entire game experience and made it even more enjoyable to play. And the best part of all, for once, my two cousins rarely had a reason or excuse to get into a fight over the plays and outcome of the game.

The actual baseball game, which Donnie and I had thoroughly enjoyed, was over. The Cardinals won over the Pirates, 7-5, moving them back to the .500 mark with a record of 4-4. Sadly, it was time for us to say our goodbyes to each other as we made our way out of the stadium. I started making my way back to the restaurant, walking on cloud nine without a care in the world.

I was feeling incredibly happy and overly excited to tell Dad all about my wonderful evening. Stepping into the restaurant, the huge smile on my face quickly vanished. Quite unexpectedly, sitting in the front section where people waited for carry-out orders, was Dad sitting alone at the table. His head was down with a very somber look plastered on his face. Looking at him intently, I quickly approached and asked, "Dad, what is wrong?

He looked up at me and soberly responded, "Grandma is gone." If you ever go from the feeling of elation and then down into the depths of deep despair within a matter of seconds, I dare and challenge you to try and keep from bawling your eyes out.

Undoubtedly, this should have been coincidentally the most happy and sad evening of my life. However, this was not to be the case. Inexplicably, twenty-three years later, I would experience another eerie and similar event.

The day was August 4, 1990. It started out with one of my friends from junior college coming to visit from Denver, Colorado. This was the year in which I had finally moved away from home, so I offered to let him stay at my apartment. Glen was this huge St. Louis sports fanatic. Whenever he came into town, we would always attend at least one St. Louis professional football, baseball, or hockey game, depending upon the time of year.

It was Saturday afternoon, and the St. Louis Cardinals were in town playing the New York Mets. Glen already had the entire day planned out. First, we would head out for the Cardinal ballgame, and he would most certainly buy himself a souvenir. After the game, we would be going over to O'Connell's, his favorite pub. Once there, we would get our fill of beer and chow down on their Saturday night special, Rib Tips. I genuinely enjoyed going there because it took me back to the old days at my family's barbecue restaurant.

We would then make our way to "Laclede's Landing," located just north of the St. Louis Gateway Arch on the Mississippi Riverfront. The "Landing" was a multi-block collection of cobblestone and vintage brick-and-cast-iron warehouses dating from 1850 through 1900. In recent years, this area on the waterfront got a facelift and converted to specialty shops, restaurants, and bars.

Right before we left for the ballgame, I gave my parents a call, "Your mother is not feeling well," said Dad. I could hear her coughing in the background. Since my friend had this big day planned out, I did not want to disappoint him. My inclination was to drive over to the house and check on her, but I did not do it.

And then, during the middle of the Cardinal ballgame, in between innings, I hear over the speakers the voice of St Louis Cardinals' longtime P.A. announcer, John Ulett. "Michael Vitale, please report to the front office desk. I was uncertain, but his voice sounded a bit mournful.

My heart skipped a beat, and my face became flushed. My anxiety hit the roof. Glen went along with me to the front office. The lady sitting there offered up no information and only gave me a very brief message. "Call Robert Vitale." I was quite puzzled by this message, and then immediately, a sense of relief overcame me. Robert was my nephew. I then recalled that he had a good friend from college who worked in public relations for the St. Louis Cardinals' front office. Robert's brother has my same name, and this other Michael Vitale was attending St Louis University at the time.

Inside my mind, it must have been necessary for me to believe everything was all right. I could not accept the thought of hearing any unwelcome news. The only thing I knew to do was alleviate myself of this overwhelming stress, and so I reasoned there was nothing wrong. I quickly surmised that this message was not for me. It was for my nephew, Michael.

I had convinced myself that Robert was just showing off to his younger brother, who must have also been attending the ballgame. He constructed this prank with his friend in the front office. They announced his brother's name, Michael

Vitale, over the P.A. system just so they could give him the message to "Call Robert Vitale."

Glen and I returned to our seats and continued having a fun time throughout the rest of the day. We did not get back to my apartment till around midnight. We reached my apartment complex parking lot and stepped out of the car, joking and laughing. From out of the shadows, my brother-in-law Mike Green appeared, catching me completely off guard. I had no idea that he had been waiting for me in the parking lot for hours. My brother-in-law, Mike, did not want me to receive the message that he was about to deliver to me over the phone.

Since he caught me by surprise, I did not give any thought as to why he would be in my parking lot at midnight. I asked with great surprise, "Mike, what are you doing here?" The thought or idea never occurred that my family had been trying to contact me all day. He looked at me very seriously and then abruptly delivered the news. "We have been trying to get a hold of you all day. Mom is gone. She passed away early this afternoon," he sadly revealed.

Immediately, I had this sense of déjà vu; this feeling of happiness and joy quickly transformed directly into the depths of my deepest despair. This was remarkably eerie in similarity to what happened to me with my grandmother's death.

It had threatened to rain all day, and I brought along an umbrella for protection against the elements. It took an amazing amount of abuse while I repeatedly threw it down into the ground with every ounce of frustration and energy. Looking up and over at my friend, Glen, I began shouting, "This is all your fault." He immediately started backing up with a frightened look written on his face.

My brother-in-law quickly spoke up. "Mike, what are you doing? That is your friend." I quickly came to my senses, realizing what a horrible thing I had just done. I profusely apologized to Glen for my terrible outburst. Handing over my apartment key, I instructed him, "Please make yourself at home. I will be back whenever possible."

I questioned and tried hard to understand or make sense of how or why two of the closest people in my life, my mother and grandmother, both passed away while I was out enjoying a St. Louis Cardinal baseball game. There was no logical explanation, so is it proper to say, "Oh, it must just be some kind of coincidence." The definition of "coincidence" is a remarkable concurrence of events or circumstances without apparent causal connection. Since there appears to be no other logical explanation, we accept and stamp it as a coincidence. Yet, there remains this haunting feeling, saying you will never really know.

***

My lone semester at St. Augustine was finally coming to an end. I never did find the right opportunity to talk or get to know my first girl crush, Cathy Sanders. Then, one Saturday afternoon, a golden opportunity was handed to me that could have changed my fate with her. In all my years spent at our restaurant, I can never recall any other time when three young girls around my age came walking into our restaurant. Let alone all by themselves, sitting down and having lunch. This was quite bold of them, and it certainly was no coincidence.

When two other girls from my class, along with Cathy Sanders, entered the restaurant, I practically wet myself in fear as to what might happen next. Quickly, I disappeared into the background, and my dad took their order for a small cheese

143

pizza and soda pops. Standing there like a frozen popsicle, I became dumbfounded and scared like a chicken as to what was happening before my eyes.

I worked away on making their pizza and stayed in the back of the restaurant until it came out of the oven. Instead of me delivering the pizza to the girls, Dad brought it over to them. After a while, I made my way out of the pizza area and crept my way back to the cash register counter. The girls were sitting at a table by the front entrance, enjoying their pizza and gabbing away as young girls would do. I am certain they saw me standing there watching them, but I was simply too shy and afraid to speak up.

I hung around in the front section, trying to look busy, with no intent on approaching them. At the same time, I could not help but wonder if this visit was purposeful or intentional. If this was intentional, then why or who instigated the whole thing? Cathy already had a boyfriend from our class named Eddie. He was very tall and skinny, but in my opinion, not so good-looking. Nevertheless, all that really mattered was for me to speak up and figure out what this was all about.

I stood there feeling quite overwhelmed and outnumbered. They may have thought I was going to entertain them, but without my backup team of Tony and Marcus, I lacked the courage. Without knowing the true circumstances behind their visit, along with their apparent disregard for me, I decided it best to keep to myself.

I was unable to think straight. All I had to do was say something like, "Hey, what are you girls doing here?" Who knows what might have happened or where the conversation might have led?

After finishing their pizza and drinks, I almost felt a bit of relief, figuring they would soon be leaving, but this was far from over. All three girls stepped up to the counter and handed me the bill. It quickly became evident they did not have enough money to pay for the meal. It was no more than about two dollars, and they only had a little over a dollar in change amongst them. I could have been this hero and let them go, and who knows how that might have turned out for me, too. Instead, the thought of them taking advantage of me seeped into my mind.

I called my dad over, never mentioning these were girls from my class. He asked if one of them could go home and get the balance from their parents. One of the girls volunteered to go home and get the balance due. The only thing I wanted was for this embarrassing fiasco to end. Cathy and the other classmate sat back down at the table, waiting for the other one to return. It felt like an eternity; if only I had decided to be kind rather than vindictive, things might have turned out differently.

Gratefully, the other girl finally returned and handed me one dollar. I handed back her change, still feeling fearful and too shy to speak up. Rather than leaving these girls with warm, good feelings about me, my guess is they departed with feelings of a bitter and regretful visit.

This encounter brought a quick end to my considering or entertaining any more thoughts of getting to know Cathy Sanders. My actions had shown and proved that I was certainly not prepared or ready for any kind of female relationship. I stood there alone, knowing what could have been instead of what would be.

***

Summer was always the time of year when our restaurant sales peaked. In the meantime, Dad had begun to devise another way of producing more income and profits out of the slabs of ribs sold. Rib tips would be an additional item on the menu. In the past, we only sold the whole slab of ribs or a half slab. The two halves on a slab of ribs are the long and short ends. The short ends were meatier, and we sold them for twenty-five cents more than the long end.

However, there is a portion of meat that you must trim off a slab of ribs to make St. Louis-style ribs. It is a strip of meat along the top of the slab of ribs. In the past, we discarded these pieces of trimmed fat and meat. Dad discovered that these pieces were known to be a very tasty treat. The Black population in the area was continuously increasing in size, and he also discovered that barbecue rib tips were a big favorite of theirs.

His new rib process included cooking the entire untrimmed slab of ribs. After the ribs cooled, he then cut off the strip along the top of the slab of ribs. Then, cut this section into smaller pieces before dropping them into a large pot of barbecue sauce on the steam table. Rib tip orders were cheaper to purchase than the long and short ends on a slab of ribs. The lower price may have also been an incentive for choosing rib tips over a slab of ribs.

This little idea created additional sales at no additional cost to us. The only problem was that our rib tips always sold out quickly. Selling out was not always a terrible thing. Sometimes, if a customer came in and discovered we sold out, they might order something else. This latest menu item also helped to increase business with the Black community in the neighborhood. And Dad was fine with that – just show him the money!

****

The school semester at St Augustine's had come to an end. Final report cards were handed out to everyone. Due in part to all my antics and poor classroom preparation, my grades had barely allowed me to pass. Thanks to Mom, I completed my homework in the second part of the semester. This might have kept me from failing seventh grade.

My two cohorts, Tony and Marcus, did not fare as well. In failing to pass, they "earned" another year in the seventh grade and quite possibly with Sister Lawrence. Tony was so upset he started crying. Marcus, however, was inconsolable and almost hysterical, crying and bawling aloud. He began pleading with Sister Lawrence to reconsider. Otherwise, his father was going to be extremely upset with him. She coldly replied, "You should have thought about that sooner. It is too late now."

I felt so badly for these two boys that I walked up to Sister Lawrence and tried to plead their case. Without a moment's notice, she swung her right arm back as far as possible. Then, she landed a blow with her hand across the side of my face.

I am thoroughly convinced that all her frustration with me during that semester came at me with this one single blow. Sister Lawrence then delivered to me one last message, "If you do not leave my classroom this very second, you will be joining them in the seventh grade." Having deserved this slap for everything caused and done over the semester, I quickly turned and walked away, never looking back to see her again.

***

I had now considered myself to be a full-fledged contributor in the preparation of food orders. I cooked hamburgers on the grill and prepared pizzas for the oven. On fried chicken orders, I would pull a half chicken from packed ice and cut it into four parts: the wing, breast, thigh, and drumstick. I coated each piece with our Golden Dip brand chicken breading. Then, I tossed each piece into the wire basket and dropped it into the deep fryer's hot oil. The barbecue pit and any items on the steam table were off-limits to me for any customer's orders. However, I did wrap up and bag all the to-go orders.

Unbelievably, there is a bit of an art in wrapping up carry-out orders. Our packaging of plates filled with food must be carefully and properly to ensure it does not fall off. First, and most importantly, you want to calculate and tear off a proper-sized piece of white butcher-type paper. This would come from one of two distinct-sized paper rolls under the steam table. After laying the paper down on the counter, the next step was to center each plate of food on top of the paper.

For me, the wrapping up of food orders could get a bit frustrating. At times, I would have difficulty tearing off the right amount of paper, either too much or too little. Next, a thin piece of wax-like paper goes over each plate of food before tightly folding the butcher paper over it. Sometimes, we would stack two or three plates on top of each other, avoiding the need to wrap each plate separately. The next step was to crisscross the paper ends that overlapped each side of the plates. Then, fold each side under the plates and wrap it tightly.

The last step is to securely place the package snugly into a paper bag. Then, fold any empty section of the paper bag underneath the plate to reinforce the package's tightness. This was a service we provided in delivering an excellent product for customers' take-out orders.

On Saturday evenings, after the dinner rush, I would head outdoors and start on my newfound weekly routine. I walked to my favorite mom-and-pop store and picked up the early edition of the Sunday Post-Dispatch newspaper. Upon my return, I would begin to prepare a meticulous dinner for myself, always making the plate of food look as perfect and enticing as possible.

One of my favorite meals began with frying up half of the chicken. I would place two pieces of cut bread onto my plate with a cup of potato salad between them. The next thing was to lay down a bunch of French fries on the plate before carefully putting the four cooked pieces of chicken (the drumstick, thigh, breast, and wing) on top of the fries. Taking my plate over to the steam table, I would dip each piece of chicken into barbecue sauce. Lastly, I grabbed a coffee cup and filled it with more barbecue sauce.

Walking into the dining room area, I made my way over to one of the tables near the television and sat down for a delicious meal. I tore a piece of chicken off the bone and dipped it into the cup of barbeque sauce, one piece at a time. I would also do the same thing with every French fry, savoring the taste of every single bite.

Looking back, as much as I thoroughly enjoyed eating all the food at our restaurant, my dad was the extreme opposite. I cannot recall him ever taking a bite of pizza, eating any fried chicken, or sitting down with a plate of barbecue ribs. He never partook in restaurant menu items.

Before leaving every morning for the restaurant, Dad would make himself breakfast. This would always include a well-beaten raw egg mixed into an extra-large cup of extremely hot coffee with cream. I would think the raw egg must have gotten cooked inside that piping hot coffee. The balance of his breakfast sustained him throughout the day.

The biggest deterrent as to why Dad never ate off the menu had to be his constant and continuous preparation of these exact same food items over and over again. He rarely sat down to enjoy a meal at the restaurant. At various times, Mom would fix him a special meal, or he might fix one for himself. It seems amazing to me how the man survived based on the small amount of food that I saw him consume.

After I completed feasting on a wonderful chicken dinner, if still free of kitchen or counter duty, I would begin making my way through the newspaper by first going through all my favorite comics. There was Blondie, Beetle Bailey, Peanuts, the Family Circle, Ziggy, and much more. After finishing the comics, I opened the Parade magazine, which had this interesting question-and-answer section. It would touch on the background and unfamiliar history of well-known celebrities and other famous individuals from past and present times. Browsing through the rest of the magazine, I sometimes encountered other articles of interest.

I went as far as checking out the financial section and looking up stock symbols of bigger companies to check out their share price. As I continued going through the newspaper, there was one thing I was astutely aware of and understood. If business started picking up or we got busy, Dad would immediately call out to me for help. Whenever this happened, it did not mean going ahead and finishing what you were doing. It meant to stop what you are doing, jump up, and get over here right now. And God help me if he spoke my name a second or third time.

Then, moving to my favorite section of the paper, I would soak up all the sports information that is of interest to me, first by going over the league standings and statistics on every single sport. Next, I would check out high-profile articles, especially those involving the St. Louis Cardinals.

When getting to the entertainment section, I first read all the reviews on movies playing at local theaters. This would sometimes help me decide whether a particular film might be of interest to me. After deciding on which movies piqued my interest, I checked out their show times with expectations of taking a trip to one of these theaters on Sunday afternoon.

The last newspaper section for me to hit was the television guide. I focused on the back section and checked out which movies were playing on television that week. I made mental notes of the ones that looked most interesting to me. There would be a range of movies dating from the 1930s into the mid-1960s. I enjoyed watching older movies just as much as the current ones, allowing me to enjoy a wider spectrum of movies.

Late weekend nights at the restaurant can get long when you arrive before noon and stay till 3 a.m. or later. Every so often, if I had enough money, I would purchase one of the cheap plastic scale models that comes in a box. Then, during those late weekend nights, I could occupy my free time by putting together a newly purchased model kit.

In the beginning, I enjoyed putting together models of various kinds of monsters from the older days: Frankenstein, Dracula, Werewolf, the Mummy, Phantom of the Opera, King Kong, and others. I then graduated to model cars, such as the Ford Mustang, Mercury Cougar, Chevrolet Corvette, Lincoln Continental, and Volkswagen Bus. The construction and completion of these scale models required purchasing additional items. Model glue was an absolute must and necessary to attach the pieces together. When I first started building models, there was no problem with my purchasing this product.

In 1959, the public began to realize kids were sniffing glue to get high, and the practice continued to grow in the 1960s. The problem got so bad that stores would no longer sell model glue to minors. Whenever I ran out of this glue, one of my parents had to go along with me to purchase the stuff.

Other items needed for these projects were model paints and brushes. This meant getting additional money to finish my model. Sometimes, I built a model and waited to complete the project until I got my next three-dollar weekly allowance. Dad gave this to me for helping at the restaurant every weekend. Completing either of these model projects would usually cost more than two dollars. The expense for an entire project required all the money I earned in a weekend; this did not matter to me.

I became thoroughly engrossed in completing these projects and enjoyed meticulously putting these models together piece by piece. Then, I would colorfully paint each model to give it a more realistic look and feel. The completion of every model left me with a sense of accomplishment. It was my creation and process in the building and finishing of these models that made it worth every penny spent.

Unfortunately for me, Mom was more than just a neat and clean freak. I would say, to a degree, she was a bit of a minimalist. At least to the degree that nothing belonged in her home without a distinct reason or purpose based upon her judgment. Anyone's purchases or belongings were susceptible to scrutinization by her and might easily become either charity or trash. The fact thirteen people were living in a limited amount of space did not help matters.

I thoroughly enjoyed building, admiring, and playing with all my models. The moment any of these models started collecting dust, mom would swoop in, and they disappeared. There also came a point in time when I stopped looking over and checking out my baseball card collection. Years later, I went searching for my collection only to discover no evidence of them anywhere. This I found to be the most egregious of all her dismissals of my property.

At the same time, I could not completely fault her. I did not take the best care of these models or make them a priority for display. Also, if my baseball cards had mattered that much to me, then I should have taken better care to secure them.

***

I can remember another customer who, without fail, came in every Saturday evening around 7 p.m. He would order anywhere from three to five fried chicken dinners. I would guess him to have been around middle age and rather short with a stocky build. At first, he kept to himself. Every so often, he would order a beer while waiting for his order to fill. I would always be hanging around the counter, taking care of other customers and food orders. After establishing himself as a weekly visitor, we started conversing a bit with each other. After that, every Saturday night, I would take a little time and chat with him to help pass the time away.

One evening, I happened to mention it seemed amazing to me that the St. Louis Theater was now in its fifty-something week of playing the same film, The Sound of Music. I complained about how ridiculous it was for one movie to be playing at the same theater for that long. At the time, there were no multi-theaters, and the local theaters changed their featured movies every week. The bigger theaters with first-run films might play there for a couple of weeks or longer if they turned out to be a big or popular hit with audiences.

I sarcastically asked this customer, "Do you think they are ever going to show another movie at that place?" As for myself, I had not yet seen it, nor had any real interest in viewing this film.

For the first time, I saw this man show off true emotion and then quickly interjected, "Oh, it's a wonderful story," he then began raving about this movie by saying it was the greatest of all time. However, the next thing he said caught me completely off guard, and I found it a bit difficult to believe. "I've been going with my family to see this movie almost every week since our first viewing of the film," he confessed.

It was not long before I got my answer as to whether another movie would play in this theater. The Sound of Music, indeed, was the last motion picture ever shown at the St. Louis Theatre. This theater would become known as Powell Hall. The St. Louis Symphony Society acquired it in 1966 through a $500,000 gift from Oscar Johnson, Jr., a longtime leader and benefactor of the Orchestra. Following an extensive $2 million renovation, the St. Louis Symphony Orchestra got its first permanent home and, to this day, is one of the world's finest concert halls. The 2689-seat Powell Hall opened on January 24, 1968.

I have made a considerable number of visits to Powell Hall, attending their symphony orchestra performances. However, I have only been there one time for the viewing of a film while it was known as the St. Louis Theater. And from what I can recall, it may well have been my very first visit to a movie theater.

It was back in 1960, and my brother Nick had only recently got his driver's license. He drove my younger sister, Maria, and me to the St. Louis theater along with his girlfriend.

He was taking us to see a re-release of the original Disney animated version of the classic film Pinocchio. When we got there, the line must have been three blocks long. I could not imagine all these people fitting into this one building. I remember looking up at a huge billboard advertising Rock Hudson and Doris Day in the classic movie, "Pillow Talk." Maria and I would later get the chance to see this movie, too. For a brief time afterward, we acted out made-up stories and pretended to be these two movie stars.

We finally made our way into the theater. As we entered the enormous seating area, I could see the movie had already begun. We started climbing and climbing up the balcony steps, and they got steeper and steeper. Turning around, I looked down and sensed a great fear of falling. It may have been vertigo or even a little bit of déjà vu. I sensed and recalled the same feeling, at less than two years old, tumbling down my basement steps at home.

We finally reached an area with empty seats in one of the last couple of rows from the top. Of course, I ended up loving this Disney classic, and the entire adventure was one of the coolest things in my young life. I took it all in, from the viewing of it on a gigantic movie picture screen to the amazing, colorful animation and the heartwarming story of a wooden puppet becoming a real boy. This experience of going into the world of movies involving unique ways of storytelling hooked me into becoming a huge movie buff for years to come.

***

The homebuilders completed the construction of our house, as promised, before the end of summer. This ensured I would begin the new school year at my designated junior high school. We moved into our new home one week prior to the start of the school year.

This did not leave me any time or a chance to check out any other kids in the neighborhood before the school year. My first day on the school bus would be my first opportunity to meet other young teenagers living near me. Maria and I waited for the bus at the designated street corner on our first day. We met up with kids in the neighborhood who came across as being very friendly.

The Catholic school that I attended, St. Casimir, was only a two or three-block walk from my home. So, this was going to be my first time riding on a school bus. As the school bus pulled up, I entered and instinctively made my way to the back of the bus. As I headed toward the very end of it, I spotted a familiar face: it was Randy Meier.

It just so happened this boy had previously attended class with me at St. Casimir school in my earlier years. He was always a leader and one of the most popular kids in class. Randy spotted me coming his way and cried out, "Oh, No." Naturally, I assumed he was joking around and everything was going along fine on the ride to school.

On the ride home, Randy, two other girls, my sister Maria, and I all got off at the same stop. We started talking and making our way down the street toward our homes. As we were walking, I discovered the other two girls were sisters, and besides that, extremely cute ones.

Quite unexpectedly, Randy turns toward me and announces, "You know, I still remember attending that birthday party of yours." He then proceeds to reveal to all of us the following tale.

At my birthday party, we played a variety of games. According to Randy, he was the winner in one of these games.

He figured that some kind of prize was due to him. I can only assume that Randy must have asked for a prize because his next statement caught me off guard. He snickered and proclaimed, "Your mother handed me a roll of toilet paper as my prize."

Both sisters began to giggle over the ending to his sordid little tale. I looked over at them with a dumbfounded look written across my face. Feeling terribly uncomfortable and quite embarrassed, I vehemently denied such a thing ever occurred, but he insisted that it did happen.

St. Angela Merici parish school and church sat tucked away inside our neighborhood. This is where my youngest brother, Rio, attended school. Adjacent to the school was a ballfield and another big playing area that was not used during weekday afternoons.

It was becoming quickly apparent that Randy still possessed this charisma about him. He was a leader in the neighborhood clique. Every day on the school bus ride home, the other neighborhood boys and girls would make plans to meet at the St. Angela of Merici ball field. While on the bus, each one of them took turns going around asking one another who was going to the school field that day. None of them, including Randy, ever asked me to join them. Herein lies two of my two biggest faults and the story of my life: pride and patience, too much of one and not enough of the other.

I was too proud and too timid to speak out and say, "I will play" or "I want to play." This same scenario played out day after day, week after week, month after month. It was excruciatingly painful to sit there and watch as they ignored me while inviting others in the neighborhood to play on the field.

Although I did manage to make friends at school, I never joined in with cliques or with any of the more popular kids. At home, I played ball in the backyard by myself or with my younger brother Rio. Sometimes, the next-door neighbor boys, who were much younger than me, joined in.

Later, I started to become friends with one of the boys in the neighborhood named Eddie. We happened to be in a couple of classes together and were becoming friends. One day, Eddie invited me to come over to his house after school. I thought this might help me to get involved with other kids in the neighborhood. We started throwing the football around on his street. Then along came Randy with Les, another boy from the neighborhood. Les attended one of the private schools, so I had never seen him before that day.

We started playing four-corner football in the street and took turns throwing the ball. We were having fun, and right then, I saw a glimmer of hope with me breaking my way into the neighborhood clique. Lester's mother stepped outside her front door and called out to him. He started talking to his mother from the street, and the conversation went on and on.

I was holding onto the football and beginning to get nervous. I needed and wanted to do something with the ball rather than just stand there. It was my turn to throw the ball, and Les was to be the recipient. Instead of throwing the ball at one of the other boys, I decided to throw a strike right at Les while he was still standing there talking with his mother. As I released the ball, I shouted, "Catch it," but it was too late.

It looked to me as if I had thrown a perfect spiral with one exception: the football hit Les smack in the face, and I squeamishly called out, "Sorry." He stared at me with a look of incredulous disbelief. The side of his face began to get redder with every second, and not simply because he was angry. His mother was still talking to him, so he was letting the mishap go. Eddie looked over at me and said, "I think you better leave before things get nasty." Thus ended my only attempt to work my way into the neighborhood clique.

***

This "toilet paper prize" story that Randy conveyed to our little group was exceedingly difficult for me to believe. It had me wondering if Mom was joking or seriously offered this to him as a prize for winning one of the birthday games. This party had taken place years earlier, so I doubted that she would recall the incident. It did not matter because I was never going to ask her the question.

Admittedly, Mom was known to play a practical joke, especially if someone had it coming. There were times when her sense of humor could be a little off-color, but it always made an impact. One such event occurred to one of my brothers-in-law, Dennis Maxwell. He had been quite a prankster in those days. There have been times when he may have gone a little too far and had a little too much fun with his practical jokes. Herein are the kinds of stunts he pulled back in his earlier days around our family.

Dennis took one of his friends, my brother Mariano, and my sister Theresa's old boyfriend Ron, on a trip into the country near his family's farm. On the car ride there, he secretly opened a small bottle of liquid that released one heck of a revolting smell. They all believed that one of the others in the car must have broken wind. It had my brother, Mariano, thinking to himself, "One of these guy's insides must be rotten."

Of course, Dennis thought this was very funny and could not keep from laughing. After a while, they figured out it was Dennis pulling off one of his pranks. I do not think the other guys thought it to be very funny, nor did they appreciate the horrible odor.

Another very annoying prank Dennis enjoyed was to lightly tap the back bumper of your car with the front of his car while driving. I considered this to be a dangerous and careless act. Yet, he would get the biggest kick out of doing this. Dennis enjoyed watching the reaction of the other person whose bumper he tapped. Of course, back in those days, car bumpers were metal, not flimsy plastic, and did not sustain any damage.

Then, one time, he placed a fake bottle of spilled ink on my mom's rug in the living room. This was one of her two formal rooms in our home, and you did not mess around in there. Dennis called my mother into the room and explained that he accidentally dropped a bottle of ink. She quickly ran and grabbed a wet cloth to attempt to soak up the spilled ink. Kneeling onto the carpet, she lightly dapped a cloth towel on the fake black plastic ink blotch. After she realized this was just another one of his pranks, Mom was fit to be tied, but Dennis kept laughing.

The worst gag may have been this one time in my mother's kitchen. Dennis called me into the room and said to me, "Do you know that it is impossible for a person to pick up an egg using only the palm of their hand?" I thought about this for a second and replied. "Dennis, you are nutty. There is nothing to it," He then dared me to prove it. The next thing I knew, he had grabbed an egg from the refrigerator and laid it down on the table.

Placing my hand directly above the egg, I prepared to pick it up and prove him wrong. Before I knew what happened, Dennis slammed his hand down on top of mine as hard as possible. Egg yolk squirted everywhere – the floor, the table, and on Mom's beautiful kitchen wallpaper. Once again, Dennis started laughing hysterically, but I do not believe anyone else thought it was very funny, especially my mother.

Knowing Mom, we figured she eventually would get the last laugh and return the favor with a gag that Dennis would never forget. During the holidays, she made her famous Sfingi, a round, light, and fluffy pastry dough fried in oil with honey poured over it. She would also add a sprinkle of sugar and crushed nuts.

Mom decided to make a special one-time batch for my brother-in-law. Taking a big bite into one of the Sfingies, he began chewing up the donut. Suddenly, he realized something did not seem right with the texture of it. "How are you enjoying that Sfingi?" asked Mom. "I added a special ingredient in there just for you…. toilet paper," she revealed.

Dennis was known to have a weak stomach for hearing any kind of bathroom conversation while eating and immediately began feeling sick. He inspected the donut only to discover she was telling the truth. All he could do was howl and complain about how this was such a vulgar joke and so very wrong. Mom was prepared for this reaction and replied, "What are you complaining about? At least I used clean paper." That was the last time my brother-in-law Dennis would ever try eating one of Mom's Sfingies or play another practical joke on her.

***

Our German Shepard dog, Vickie, was just over a year old the first time that she was "in heat" through the fertility cycle. It was also the first time for me to witness animals mating. I cannot explain why I found it funny, but Timber, our giant dog, was riding Vickie on her back. I remember that our waitress, Mary, had found this to be revolting, and she almost felt sorry for poor Vickie. Mary's reaction just made the whole thing seem even funnier to me.

After that, I began watching with anticipation as Vickie progressed toward the birth of her first puppies. Dad was just as happy and excited, desperately wanting to see what a mixed breed of German Shepherd and Giant Alaskan Malamute would deliver to him. It was beginning to get very cold in the evenings. So, Dad added hay to the floor inside of a makeshift doghouse, along with a heat lamp to warm it up.

It was on a Saturday evening when I watched in amazement and fascination while Vickie gave birth, one at a time, to a dozen puppies. The normal litter size can range from 1 to 12 puppies. Since there were so many, I have no doubt these puppies were much smaller in size than those having a lesser number in the litter.

We were so happy and excited when our dog, Vickie, produced such a large litter of pups. What we failed to understand is she was barely over one year old. The next day, we arrived at the restaurant a little before noon. I rushed into the backyard, anxious to check on the puppies. Peering inside the doghouse, I was unable to locate any of the pups and kept looking around, trying to figure out where they could be hiding. I searched long and hard, trying to find the whereabouts of just one puppy. Seeking help, I called out to Dad for assistance. With his hands, he began rummaging through the bed of hay and found nothing.

An inexperienced mother dog may not recognize her puppies as being her offspring. Newborn puppies move erratically and make high-pitched sounds. These behaviors mimic the actions of prey animals, such as mice. If a female dog devours her puppies, it usually occurs immediately after birth or in a matter of a day or two later. There are varied reasons why mothers will do this. It is not exclusive to one breed.

It seemed curious to me that our dog gave birth and was responsible for the lives of twelve puppies. This just so happened to be the same number that Dad had to support financially at one time. Is it possible that our dog, Vickie, found this amount to be too overwhelming? I know there were times when the demands and pressure of life would get to be too much for Dad. I would sometimes discover him in the far corner of the kitchen. After retrieving a bottle of whiskey kept hidden on a back shelf, he would take a big swig right out of the bottle.

We both were quite upset and disappointed once it became evident to us Vickie had eaten her puppies. However, we understood this was by no means a malicious act. It was merely an act of ignorance. Dad promised himself not to allow puppies ever to be born again in that yard.

(The 7th Inning)

---1967---

My role in doing anything overly exciting on a Friday evening, Saturday, or Sunday afternoon became limited to my activities in and around our restaurant. This was my escape from the realities of school and my non-existent after-school activities. Unfortunately, this left me with an extremely disappointing and helpless feeling surrounding my high school years. Eventually, my part in working at the restaurant would be an excuse and reason never to try out for after-school sports.

Besides that, I really did not consider myself an extremely athletic person. There were never any great opportunities for me to get involved in organized sports. This may have contributed to my lack of speed, agility, and coordination. Although I possessed a tall and bulky frame with a good build, equality in muscular strength was not happening. Part of all sports activities and their practices would occur on weekends, which made it easier for me not to participate. Simply put, Dad needed my help at the restaurant on weekends, and I made it my place to be there.

I kept busy at the restaurant on Friday nights and all day on Saturdays. However, our Sunday business was getting slower, along with the early part of the week. The Black community in the neighborhood was continuing to grow, and carry-out orders were now exceeding our dining room sales. I can only surmise the Black customers in the neighborhood still felt a bit intimidated by the white crowd inside the dining room area and were sticking with ordering carry-out.

It was obvious this underlying issue was contributing to the major transition in our neighborhood economy. The white middle-class and higher-income individuals had moved out of the area. This left the neighborhood with a larger amount of lower-class, lower-income individuals. In addition, the continued growth of the Black population in the area had continued to lower the neighborhood income range.

Our Sunday business was slowing, but we were still getting a steady stream of customers throughout the day. However, it was something that Dad and our waitress, Mary, could easily manage by themselves. This gave me an opportunity to take off on my own and enjoy part of the afternoon. The local Northside movie theater was only five or six blocks away. Unfortunately, it was quickly falling into a bit of disarray. The audience inside the place had become more reflective of the immediate area. It was now me who felt intimidated by the crowd of people inside the theater, and I no longer felt comfortable going in there.

In making my way toward Grand Avenue, a new alternative was taking a bus ride south for about two miles. This took me to midtown St. Louis. This area of the town had movie theaters, restaurants, St. Louis University, and St Francis Xavier College Church. My main purpose in taking this bus ride was to attend the Fabulous Fox Theater.

The movie pioneer William Fox had this theater built as a showcase for films coming from the Fox Film Corporation and the addition of various elaborate stage shows. It was one of a group of five spectacular Fox Theatres built by Fox in the late 1920s. The other cities were Brooklyn, Atlanta, Detroit, and San Francisco.

Tragically, they demolished the Brooklyn Fox Theater in the 1960s, and the one located in San Francisco came down during the 1970s. The other building went under renovation and survived into the present to become a versatile performing arts venue. Surprisingly, the Fox Theater in Atlanta still had a segregated entrance for Black people that stayed active until 1962, when the theater slowly desegregated.

The Fabulous Fox Theater in St. Louis opened in 1929, costing six million to build, and was the second-largest theater in the United States with 5,060 seats. The architecture inside the building, just like its name, was fabulous. It had been one of St. Louis's leading movie theaters through the 1960s.

Upon my first visit, I realized there was no other theater that could compare its delivery and presentation to the viewing of a movie production. The massive size of this theater and its gigantic screen was awe-inspiring. The better the film, the greater my enjoyment. Although I might have been going there only to watch a movie, for me, it was more like going to a special event.

The Fabulous Fox Theater was fast approaching the waning years of its movie house existence. At times, there might be less than two or three hundred people inside the theater, and I would get the sense of being alone inside this enormous place. However, it certainly did not take anything away from my experience or the impact I felt from viewing movies inside this exquisite palace.

As much as I enjoyed my trips going to the Fabulous Fox, back in those days, there were other great movie houses around the midtown and downtown areas. On Sundays, I would also make trips to other places like the Ambassador Theater, Lowe's State, and Lowe's Mid City. The St. Louis Theater had already closed. It was going through renovation to become the St. Louis Symphony Hall. None of these other movie showcases could touch the eloquence or class inside of The Fabulous Fox.

***

Around this same time, a young Black man came into our restaurant every day. Arthur was his name, but we all just called him Art. I would guess him to be somewhere around thirty years old. He was tall, very thin, well-groomed, and wore glasses. There was also something a little different about him. I am quite certain that he lived with his parents in one of the houses located near the restaurant.

Art would come into our place, sometimes twice a day, and get a cup of coffee with cream and sugar. There was no need for him to order because he got the same thing every single time. He would sit at the lone table next to the front entrance. Art would sit there staring out the window or into space for around an hour or so. He was always very courteous and respectful and was neither deaf nor dumb but simply chose not to speak. There were times when Art would stay away from home too long. Then, his mother would come up to our place and take him back home.

There was no way for me to know, but looking back, Art more than likely had a form or type of autism. Whatever his mental situation might have been, it was incredibly sad to see this young, clean-cut-looking Black man wasting away. Mom,

167

Dad, and I became very fond of him. For the next couple of years, Art became somewhat of a permanent fixture in our place.

One day, he failed to show up, and we never heard from him again. I really had no way to go about inquiring as to what happened. He never spoke to anyone who came into our place, and his mother was the only one we knew connected to him. Mom and Dad told me that the family had moved away. I always wondered if they knew this or simply assumed it.

***

The time had come for my sister, Theresa, to take center stage in our family. She was to be the next in line to be married. The man of her dreams had recently immigrated to the United States from Sicily. Vince Monteleone had learned and perfected the art of fine tailoring. Like so many other immigrants, he came to this country with the hope and expectation of building his fortune for a better life.

He learned to speak the English language very quickly, mainly through the time spent with my sister. This slender, dark, handsome Scillian knew how to be charming. His personality would later help in contributing to the success of his future tailoring business and shop. Vince wisely left the managing of household and business affairs to my sister, making them a perfect team.

On the day of their wedding, it was an extremely hot one. My parents, one more time, would do the catering of the wedding reception held in a church banquet hall. Although everything that day came off without a hitch, the latter part of that evening would prove to be rather curious and unusual.

Mr. Monteleone, Vince's father, was a much older man and had only been in our country for a brief time. He carried with him traditions from the old country. With that in mind, he approached my father with a special request or, at the very least, a suggestion. Dad felt none too excited about his proposal, but to relieve this old man's concerns, he agreed to go along with it.

After leaving the wedding, Theresa and Vince began their drive home to their new apartment, with both fathers following in the car behind them. I can only imagine the conversation that must have taken place between the bride and groom. After arriving home, the happy couple made their way to the front door with the two fathers trailing directly behind them.

As they reached the front door, both fathers entered first. They started checking inside the closets, then under the couch and bed. In Sicily, there were unsavory individuals who lay in wait for unsuspecting newlywed couples. Then, they would attempt to take the couple by surprise and their possession of envelopes filled with money. Where Mr. Monteleone lived, this kind of act would be a safety measure.

Dad was feeling a bit embarrassed over this privacy intrusion and apologized to my sister. Theresa understood his reasoning for going along with the whole charade and quickly put his mind at ease, "Dad, it is fine, no big deal, really," she insisted. The two older men went about checking out the apartment to their satisfaction. Afterward, the newlywed couple thanked both fathers for their welfare and concern before sending them on their way.

Shortly after my sister Theresa's wedding, it was my brother Nick's turn. He had gotten engaged to the love of his life, Joannie Hines, shortly before getting drafted. After Nick finished his one-year duty in South Korea, he returned to the

States. While on leave from the army, Nick and Joan planned to go forward with their marriage plans and became one.

They had a beautiful church ceremony, then afterward, a private dinner celebration for the immediate family members. The army had promoted Nick to the status of Sergeant and stationed him at Fort Campbell in Kentucky. This promotion allowed them to receive government housing as a married couple. They were now able to begin their lives together as husband and wife.

***

I can only recall one time ever catching my dad acting irrationally. It was the middle of the night, and we were driving home from the restaurant. For whatever reason, our waitress, Mary, was not riding along in the car with us on that night. As we made our way down Interstate I-70, there was almost no one else on the road. I suddenly noticed that Dad was driving a little bit faster than normal. This continued for a brief period, and then he began driving even faster. Looking over at the speedometer, I could see us going well above the speed limit of 55 m.p.h. As he began going even faster, I started thinking to myself, "Dad has never driven this fast before."

A bit of concern entered my mind when I noticed the speedometer reached 80 m.p.h. As he continued to keep his foot down on the pedal, I could not decide whether to stare at the road or the speedometer, so I kept flashing my eyes back and forth. We were now traveling at a speed of over 90 m.p.h. and approaching the century mark. A sense of fear quickly came over me. The speedometer crossed over 100 m.p.h., and we were flying down that road. Then, within an instant, Dad abruptly took his foot off the accelerator.

There were times in the past when he scared or unnerved me, but this was something different. I was shocked and confused, having never experienced this type of behavior from him. For whatever reason, I chose not to question or say a word about the whole incident. The fact he stopped pushing the limits was all that mattered to me.

Everything tells me that Dad was the definition of a selfless family man, always putting the needs of his family ahead of his own. For that matter, there was a time when his needs did not seem to exist. He labored twelve to sixteen hours a day throughout his married life, and yet never did I hear him utter words like, "I need a little time for myself. I need to get away."

Is it possible he simply wanted to see how it felt to drive over 100 m.p.h.? I wondered if he had ever taken the time to do something exciting in his life. As far as I knew, the only thing he ever made time available for was family and work.

I suppose that one pleasure Dad got out of life besides our family was his dogs. The itch for another dog had taken over again, and this time, he acquired a full-grown Doberman Pinscher with the name Mike. I thought to myself, "Wait a minute, that's my name," but Dad said we should keep it so as not to confuse the dog. This breed of dog has outstanding traits, but two stood out above the others: bravery and fearlessness. The previous owner used him as a guard dog for protection against intruders. I never got the chance to make a connection with Mike.

Once this purebred Doberman entered our yard, it did not take but a moment for Timber to start exercising his territorial dominance. This dog was not about to get intimated or dominated by this humongous dog, and the two of them started going after each other. Dad figured within a couple of days, they would get tired of fighting and learn to build a relationship with one another.

Their immediate hatred for one another did not stop. The two of them would continue fighting off and on throughout the day. The rivalry between them was becoming vicious and getting out of hand. After about a week or so of Mike's arrival in the yard, Dad had no other choice but to separate the two of them. There was another section of the yard with a separate gate located behind the dining room area of the building. Dad felt it would be best, for now, to move Mike into that area.

Although the two dogs were in different sections of the yard, it did not really help the situation all that much. Mike would bark voraciously, showing all his teeth from behind the gate. Timber would come running up to the gate, bellowing right back at him.

This went on for another week or so. I suppose Dad was in a bit of a quandary on what more he should do. If I had to guess, I would say our neighbors in the apartment flats behind us were none too happy. The fighting going on between these dogs would continue throughout the night. And then, something very curious happened one night after closing. Someone had taken the initiative to unlock the gate that separated these two dogs.

When Dad returned the next day, he found it to be noticeably quiet inside the backyard. He walked out into the yard to investigate. After reaching the back section of the yard, Dad found the back gate open. There lying on the ground was Mike, motionless but still breathing.

This poor dog had bites all over his body, and Timber showed no signs of any bites or scratches. His coat was so thick that even a Doberman's teeth could not penetrate it. Dad was devastated and felt awful over what had transpired. His bodily injuries were too severe, and he did not recover.

Other people in the neighborhood may have gotten wind of this dogfight. It could have been a neighbor or the person who let the two dogs go at each other. Whatever the case, shortly after this dog fight incident occurred, Timber went missing.

There was a lock on the gate, but the perpetrators pulled up the fence from the bottom and somehow lured Timber out of the yard. Now, here comes the confusing and crazy part of this whole incident. Within a day or two after Timber went missing, we found him right back in our yard. Somehow, whoever took him decided to bring this dog back to us.

We did not know if they had stolen or kidnapped him. Allow me to explain. Dad figured they might have kidnapped him to fight against other dogs. It did not appear that he was in any fights, but with this dog, it was impossible to tell. However, I believe if that were the case, then why would they kidnap and return him?

A more likely scenario would have been that neighborhood boys took him, and the parents made them bring him back. Either way, I do not think Dad heeded the warning or took the necessary precautions to avoid this happening again. The next time they took Timber from the yard, he never returned.

Timber stolen from the yard twice was, for me, both a pivotal sign and a warning of how drastically this neighborhood had changed. An even more obvious sign was the robberies that were beginning to occur within the neighborhood. This included all the local mom-and-pop shops, taverns, dairy, and hardware stores.

These occurrences were not simply due to the Black population moving into the neighborhood. The true culprits were low-income, unemployed, or near-poverty-stricken individuals moving into the area, whether they be black or white. Whenever this type of class element comes into the neighborhood, it is immediately followed by drugs and crime. I am certain these types of individuals did not have enough money to eat or feed their drug addictions. In desperation, these people will do whatever is necessary to fulfill their needs.

***

One truly bright spot in this year, for me anyway, had to be witnessing the St. Louis Cardinals winning 101 games en route to the National League pennant. The team featured All-Stars: Orlando Cepeda (selected the National League Most Valuable Player), Lou Brock, Tim McCarver, and 1964 World Series MVP Bob Gibson. The Red Sox had reached the World Series by emerging victorious in a dramatic four-team pennant race. This team was led by the American League Triple Crown winner Carl Yastrzemski and ace pitcher Jim Lonborg, winner of the American League Cy Young Award.

In a rematch of the 1946 World Series, the Cardinals won in seven games. This was their second world championship in four years and eighth overall. It was also the first World Series since 1948 that did not include either the Yankees, Dodgers, or Giants.

(The 8th Inning)

---1968---

Our family had now become less than half its size of thirteen, and economically, that was a good thing. Although sales from our restaurant were still coming in near our previous levels, it was only because of the opening of Sundays, the twice-hiked menu prices, and the addition of Rib Tips to the menu. The actual profit from the restaurant sales was a much lesser amount.

Our waitress, Mary, had three sons: Art, the oldest, worked in accounting after graduating from business school and had moved away from the St. Louis area. The second son, Jimmy, stopped attending high school. He had found full-time work and was not around the home all that much. Mary was not thrilled with the idea of always having to leave her third son, Johnny, alone at home. On the weekends, Dad gave her permission to bring him along and hang out at the restaurant.

Johnny was around thirteen years old, two years younger than me. We spent time together at the restaurant whenever there would be a slowdown in business during the day. Sometimes, we walked around the neighborhood, but always with explicit instructions from our parents not to stray too far away. My main purpose for being at the restaurant on weekends was still to help whenever needed.

I did not always agree with Johnny's thought process of our world. He was bitter and very skeptical about the brighter side of things in life. This, in part, may have come from our different family upbringing. He came from a broken home with no father, and they lived in one of the poorer areas of town. His two brothers were older and no longer around. Besides that, his mother was always working. However, under the circumstances, I believe Mary had done her level best in raising her three boys.

Johnny was the kid who introduced me to cigarette smoking. During these times, and given my age, it seemed like a cool thing to do. Throughout the country, cigarette smoking was as popular as ever. I figured it must be something worth trying since it appealed to so many and appeared to give people real pleasure. Being underage, we only got the chance to perform this act in secrecy. It also gave us another good reason to leave the restaurant and go for a walk.

One very cold winter's day, Johnny and I threw on our coats and went out for a quick walk to smoke a cigarette. We were still finishing off our smokes as we neared the first house to the left of the restaurant. This was the house where Phil Polizzi had lived, and it is now occupied by his son, Vince, and daughter-in-law, Sonja. I knew her very well because she happened to be one of our former waitresses.

As we approached the house, we noticed Sonja coming out of the front porch door. We both immediately cuffed our cigarettes behind the palms of our hands. We did not want her spotting us holding a lit cigarette due to the risk she might say something. I went as far as sticking my hand with the burning cigarette inside my coat pocket.

We spoke to her briefly and then quickly moved on. I froze in my tracks when stunned by the head of a deer sitting atop their fence post. I could only assume that Vince Polizzi must have shot a deer and was displaying his trophy. I personally thought it to be a truly crude and obscene act of sportsmanship. We reached the entrance to my restaurant and quickly put out the cigarettes before entering.

I sensed the smell of something burning. It did not take long for me to realize my coat pocket was hot and smoldering. A piece of hot ash from the cigarette must have fallen into the lining of my coat pocket. I rushed to pour water inside the pocket and stopped it from burning any further. From that day on, every time I attempted to put something into that pocket with a hole inside of it, I cursed and recalled my dumb yet necessary maneuver.

Fortunately, cigarette smoking was never a great desire of mine, nor did I ever feel addicted. The funny thing about that is I continued this habit. It was something to do, and it would give me moments to reflect or escape. Sometimes, it was just a way of breaking up the monotony of each day. When I was in my thirties, Dad retired and thought it would be best if he quit smoking for health reasons, not to mention the ridiculous money wasted on smoking these cancer sticks.

He struggled at great length in attempting to completely break himself away from cigarettes. I was still living at home and knew my smoking around him was not making it any easier to quit. I figured it was a smart idea to quit myself, and it would also make the process easier for Dad to quit. Using this strategy, we both successfully kicked the filthy habit for good.

***

There were robberies continuously taking place at the businesses inside our neighborhood. When we first took over the restaurant, there were never any occurrences of robberies or break-ins. Dad was concerned and thought that he should become more prepared for anyone who might want to consider robbing our place. The Colt 45 long barrel came from the hidden compartment under the cash register and went directly inside his pant waist belt, behind his long white apron.

More than anything else, he wanted to send a powerful message to anyone coming inside to case the joint: "I'm ready for you." In other words, if you come here looking to rob my place, it will not be a walk in the park or a piece of cake. Dad was making it noticeably clear that they were going to have a fight on their hands.

After that, I began to imagine things like someone walking through our door, holding a gun, and attempting to rob our place. My bigger concern was how Dad was going to react and deal with the situation. It left me in constant fear and chance of this forthcoming event.

I began to think that things could not get any worse but then came the assassination of Dr. Martin Luther King Jr. Although the riots and firebombings were happening throughout major cities in retaliation for King's death, there were other reasons for all these conflicts. Although segregation was illegal, discriminatory housing policies, the white flight to suburbs, and income disparities were pushing Black urban residents into low-income housing areas. These areas were often poorly maintained, and the Black community was underemployed, not to mention their being hassled by local police.

I will never forget this one Saturday afternoon when two large and very hefty-looking Black women came into our restaurant. They were sitting quietly at the lone table by the front entrance and enjoying a plate of barbecue ribs. On the payphone directly across from them was this very skinny young white guy. I noticed these two women were beginning to raise their voices. They were none too happy with the foul language the young man was using over the phone.

"You better watch your mouth. This ain't no place for that kind of language," one of the women pointed out to him. Soon afterward, the guy hung up the phone and, staring over at these two women, replied, "You best mind your own business."

From there, things really heated up. Suddenly, the two women jumped up out of their seats. One of them reared back and popped him in the face with her fist while the other one raised her fork high into the air, ready to take a stab at him. I stood at the counter frozen, too stunned to react or even speak. Out of the corner of my eye, I spotted Dad spring into action and quickly positioned himself between the two women and the young guy.

He was bleeding badly from his mouth and nose. "Go wash yourself off," said Dad, directing the young guy over to the wash basin next to the restrooms. These women were not yet satisfied; this punk had sparked a fire under them, and they felt disrespected. The two women were much bigger than Dad and instructed, "You need to kick his skinny ass outta here."

"All right, all right, that's enough. Let's just calm down and finish your lunch," Dad suggested. He then gestured them back to their table, but these women would not budge. Instead, they turned around and stormed out of the restaurant, complaining the entire way out.

I stood behind the counter, trying to catch my breath while taking in everything that had just happened. The next thing I knew, two big, strong-looking Black men came rushing into the place looking for this fellow. Meanwhile, this skinny young guy was still busy cleaning himself up at the water basin. He caught them out of the corner of his eye and quickly darted into the men's restroom.

Once again, in a flash, Dad goes running past these two Black men. Tagging along behind them were the same two women with a couple of little kids in tow. Dad stood in front of the bathroom door, blocking their way with his Colt 45 still tucked inside his belt buckle and apron.

Feeling terrified, I immediately grabbed hold of the phone and called the police. I stood there thinking all the while, "What in the world is my dad standing in front of that bathroom door in the way of four very large, strong, and angry-looking people?" I thought to myself, he must be crazy but also tough and courageous. Fortunately, or maybe unfortunately, I did not appear to have inherited any of those traits. Still, I could not help but admire him for willingly protecting this frightened little guy.

While all this was happening, two more little kids came running into the place screaming, "He's getting away out the window!" Our men's and women's restrooms each had this small double window. If you had fully raised the bottom window to the top, it might have provided an opening a little more than a foot in height and width. Somehow, this little, skinny, scrawny guy managed to squeeze his way through that opening.

Upon hearing of the escape, this small mob went trotting out the front door, chasing after him. He must have successfully escaped because they came back to our place still very unhappy. Thankfully, the police arrived about the same time as this angry little group made their return. After a while, cooler heads prevailed, and the incident ended peacefully.

I was quite relieved to see this debacle had finally ended. However, it got me to wondering. If that guy had not fled out the window, how would this have all played out? God is always there and watching over my family. Yet, I still wondered if this was only the beginning of what was ahead for my dad in his attempt to keep this business up and running. He had lived and worked in this kind of environment dating back to his younger days with his father in the tavern and bootleg business.

As for me, attending Catholic school and going to mass every day before school is the way Mom raised us. In my early years at Catholic school, I took religion seriously and closer to my heart than most other children. My inner faith, along with the strong religious influence from Mom and my siblings, helped sculpt me into a gentle, peaceful young man. I would always feel embarrassed and out of place for not stepping up whenever things started getting hairy or out of control. Even so, I continued working at Dad's side, trying to do my best to suppress all concerns and fears.

***

It was right around this same time that I came across something I had never witnessed before. A Black person around thirtyish came walking through our front entrance and sashayed their way up to the front counter. The first thing I noticed was their hairstyle looked fancy but too short for a female. The face makeup was thick and caked onto the skin. This person had covered themselves in jewelry and rings on their fingers with long painted nails. The clothing seemed irrelevant to me since it did nothing to help accentuate their body. I then hear this weird-sounding voice coming out of this person, adding even more confusion to my mind.

As I took down the food order, I could not stop myself from staring at this person. I kept trying to figure out if this was a man or a woman. While the order was being prepared, I spent a good part of the time trying to decide. Although I knew all about gay people, this was something vastly different from that.

This person was genuinely nice and friendly toward me. It would not be the only visit to our restaurant, so I had more time to make my final decision on their gender. After coming back repeatedly, it became fairly evident to me this was a man. However, he was doing everything possible to give off the appearance of a woman.

In our country, there have been discussions, concerns, and differences of opinion about a person's freedom or right to choose to be whatever they want to be. It is not our place to judge people on the way they feel or what they choose to do with their bodies. However, the fact remains that I was unaware of this kind of practice. Yet, in observing how this person appeared to me and what he did to himself, it seemed inherently and biologically confusing and wrong. To this day, it causes me to have concerns over the principal issues and controversy surrounding the transgender movement.

****

The Fourth of July, our country's celebrated Independence Day, was fast approaching. Everyone loves this holiday, but it was not exactly one of Mom's favorite times of the year. The reason behind her dislike was all those fireworks, especially firecrackers. I loved shooting off and messing around with fireworks. She pleaded and warned my older brother, Nick, and me about the dangers of these mini dynamite sticks. We paid no heed to her warnings. The thrill of booming sounds from firecrackers going off and seeing fireworks bursting in the air, showing off colorful illuminations and designs, was too enticing to ignore or avoid.

Mom's tragic story did not persuade me to buy and shoot off these loud, explosive gadgets. The tragic story is related to the death of her ten-year-old stepbrother, Gioacchino. When she was only three years old, he shot off a firecracker, which blew up in his hand. The injury was improperly treated and developed into a lockjaw. This came on suddenly, and the symptoms can peak within hours. There was no antibiotic available in those days for this type of bacterial infection, and Gioacchino did not survive.

Johnny was spending another one of his Saturdays at our restaurant. We both were hanging around outside of the restaurant, playing with firecrackers. We kept trying to devise unusual ways to shoot them off and watch them explode. One of Johnny's brilliant ideas was to light a firecracker and throw it into the air as high and as far as possible. The purpose and expectations were to watch it blow up mid-flight. There happens to be one problem with this brilliant idea. To execute this plan, you first need to hold onto the lit firecracker till the last possible moment. The firecracker wicks were long, so it really came down to the proper timing of the release.

On one of these attempts, Johnny offered up the suggestion of me reaching back with my arm behind my back as far as possible. He would get behind me, light the wick, and then give me the signal to throw it up before the lighted wick reached the firecracker. So, there I was, standing and waiting for his signal to throw the firecracker while the wick started to burn down. This required a great amount of trust on my part. As the wick continued burning down, I began to get extremely nervous and wanted to let the thing fly. Finally, my nerves could not hold out any longer, and three things occurred simultaneously: I threw the firecracker, Johnny shouted out, "Throw it," and the firecracker exploded.

A thunderous noise reverberated through my head. I felt the heat and sting of the explosion in my hand. I never saw the explosion; I only heard it. Johnny, standing a fair distance away, had a front-row view of the entire thing and thought the whole thing was hilariously funny. Looking down at my hand, I could see what looked like a gunpowder burn. The skin between my thumb and forefinger had gunpowder residue and was very red and sore to the touch. I could still feel the stinging and throbbing in my hand.

Although I was certain that the firecracker did not blow up in my hand, it certainly came dangerously close when it exploded. To say the least, I was none too happy with Johnny holding off so long before telling me to throw it. After that stunt, I became quite skeptical of anything he ever said or suggested to me.

I did not want to show Mom or Dad my slightly burned hand, especially because of how it had happened. Instead, I decided to vigorously wash my hands and keep a close eye on the slight gunpowder burn. I felt very paranoid over the next couple of days, frequently checking out my hand. At the same time, I kept recalling Mom's story about her brother and my own careless stupidity. This little experiment with the firecracker made it clear to me that fireworks are truly nothing to mess around with, and you should always use extreme caution. Strangely enough, this little scare did not stop me from continuing the practice of shooting off fireworks or firecrackers.

***

After persistent but friendly persuasion, Dad finally agreed to let me drive the car home late at night after closing. I thought it was a great idea because there was truly little traffic on the road. This went on for weeks. He began feeling comfortable with my driving ability and would fall asleep on the ride home. It made me feel good knowing Dad got himself a little extra rest while I took care of things. This routine of driving home on the weekends after closing would continue after passing my driver's test.

Around this same time, I was attending a driver's education class at my high school. This consisted of classroom participation, one day a week in a simulation machine, and one day a week driving in the car. There was always an instructor and two other students in the car. All three students would get their turn to drive in an area near the school.

One afternoon, it was my turn to drive, and everything about my driving was going smoothly. As we drove down this one rural road, I noticed a dog sitting on top of a mound alongside the road. It was sitting there quietly as we approached and got closer. As I was about to pass by, the darndest thing happened. This dog, looking as if it shot out of a cannon, ran onto the road directly in front of us. There was absolutely no time for me to react. Our car ran directly over this poor, unfortunate creature.

Suffice it to say, I felt awful. As I glanced into the rearview mirror, I spotted looks of disdain coming my way from the two students in the back seat. From the expression on their faces, they were ready to convict me guilty of murder. The instructor quickly spoke up to say, "Do not concern yourself. There was nothing you could have done. That dog jumped right out in front of our car."

The teaching instructor was correct in his assessment of this event. However, I failed to learn at that moment what this event tried to teach me during this driving school ride. You should always be prepared and cautious. The only way to do this is by expecting the unexpected.

***

One Saturday afternoon, while hanging around the food counter, I noticed Dad had been inside the men's restroom for a lengthy amount of time. Just as I was about to check and make sure everything was all right, the restroom door sprang open. He proceeded to thoroughly wash his hands before tying back on his long white apron. Making his way toward the counter, I could hear him muttering something under his breath. He then took a deep breath and blew it out loudly.

He looked over at me and passed along these unforgettable words, "Nothing in life is easy. Sometimes, it is even hard to take a crap." I snickered for a moment at the thought of Dad working that hard to relieve himself. At the same time, I was not sure if he was trying to be funny or deadly serious. It did make one thing clear to me, and that was how Dad must have been feeling about life's treatment. He may have been living a good life, but it was also a tough one. In his mind, did everything in life seem like one big continuous struggle, all the way down to his bodily functions?

***

One Saturday evening, Dad came walking out of this very same restroom and bumped into this young Black man coming toward him from the other direction. After they bumped into each other, Dad touched and pushed off the young man's shoulder while saying, "Pardon me." The man stopped in his tracks and turned around, calling out rhetorically, "Pardon me?" He then attempted to correct my dad's grammar, "You're not supposed to say pardon me; you say excuse me."

Dad gave the man a puzzled look. Although irritated by this remark, he attempted to ignore the comment. Once again, the person announced, "It's excuse me, not pardon me," and he began drawing closer. I cannot say or know what motivated this man to react in this manner. What I did know was that my dad was certainly not going to bow down to his relentless demand. He looked at the man one more time and replied, "I said pardon me; drop it."

Dad walked away and went behind the front counter stand. This person became even more enraged and continued to rant on. Finally realizing that no satisfaction would be coming his way, he exited our place with a huge scowl etched on his face.

It did not take too long before we heard a thundering "BOOM" up against our building. I stood there stunned, with no idea what might have caused such a noise and disturbance. I then heard Dad shout out, "What the hell!" Within a matter of seconds, another "BOOM" shot up against our building. We both immediately thought, "It has got to be that young Black man who was in here causing a scene."

It might have been a gun, and it may have been something else we did not know. However, Dad was certainly smart enough to know it could have been a gun, and he certainly was not going out the front door to investigate. Instead, he took hold of the Colt 45 stuck in his waist and went out the back door into the yard. I followed behind him, but he stopped and turned around, ordering me, "Stay back here." Dad made his way to the front side of the yard, and staying behind our large dumpster, he peered around its side, attempting to find the location of this man.

It was very dark around the area of the dumpster where he was standing. I could not make out what he was doing, and there was only one thought and concern in my mind. What if Dad spots this guy and takes a shot at him? Thankfully, after a minute or so, he gave up trying to locate the whereabouts of this nut job. Making his way back to where I was waiting, we headed back inside the restaurant.

It is possible this man simply was getting all that pent-up anger out of his system and then fled. It is also possible that he thought better about what he was doing and decided to take off. Another possibility could have been this man was waiting for Dad to come out the front door so he could take a shot at him. I am quite certain this man never again entered our door.

I cannot recall whether we bothered to check for damage to the building on the following day. Whatever the case, a sense of relief came over me once it became evident the threat was over. However, I could not help but wonder about the number of incidents that would occur before something awful happened.

***

It was the middle of summer; Johnny Stephens had stopped making his weekend visits to our restaurant. In part, this was due to a job he obtained at Busch Stadium II. This was the new home of the St. Louis Cardinals. Upon hearing about the job, it piqued my interest, and I had to know more details.

The position was that of a "stand boy" working at one of the ballpark concession stands. Dad only required me to work at the restaurant on weekends. I began considering the possibility of getting one of those jobs. I figured that he might let me work there on a weekday or weeknight when the Cardinals were playing in town.

"Hey, Dad, how about letting me go for one of those stand-boy jobs?" I politely pleaded. "Why do you want that job?" he questioned. "To make some money, and it might be fun working at the ballpark," I explained. Dad could not argue with me taking the initiative to make extra money for myself, although he was already paying me $5.00 a week. I just hoped it would not upset him that I wanted to leave our restaurant to work somewhere else. "If you want to do this, go ahead," he confirmed.

The stand-boy job was an open-ended position. You go through a specific entrance before each game at the stadium and print your name on a sign-in sheet. If you got there early enough, and there were still open spots, then you were in. During the game, my main duty was making trips down to the commissary in the lower level. This was my destination whenever the concession stand looked to be running low on certain products and menu items.

Stand-boys would stay in the back room of the concession stand during a fair portion of the game. One other good thing about this job was that there were concession stands with a back room with a small opening a couple of feet above the floor. From here, you could get a partial view of the field and watch the game.

After the ballgame, I would wait for the other concession employees to vacate. Then, I swept the floors and did a complete inventory count for every product item in the concession stand. I first counted all unused beer cups, soda cups, and popcorn holders. Then, I counted any remaining soft pretzels, hot dogs, hamburgers, buns, and any other remaining snack products. My job was to ensure that I had accounted for every item in the concession stand.

I waited for this motorized cart to come by, pick up the remaining product, and take my inventory sheet for delivery to the commissary. Then, later, they verified the total number of items sold along with the inventory count of all unused products. In doing this, they forced all concessionaires to be honest and avoid stealing or giving away product items for free.

The new Bush Stadium II was in downtown St. Louis. I would get there by taking a short bus ride from our restaurant. Night games started around 8 p.m. It was usually somewhere around midnight before finishing the job. Since the bus I took did not run that late at night, Dad would drive over and pick me up. At this point, the restaurant was closing by midnight since our extremely late weeknight business had become almost nonexistent.

I did this job for the remainder of the summer and would receive a check for $7.50 per game. Also, I had the opportunity to work at one World Series game. This was quite exciting and the only time I have ever attended one in person. A week later, a letter came in the mailbox for me. Surprisingly and happily, it was a $10.00 check for that game.

The St. Louis Cardinals played the Detroit Tigers in the 1968 World Series, and it went to seven games. The final game was in Detroit, and I watched it on my television from home. In this game, Bob Gibson allowed three runs on four straight hits in the seventh inning. He lost to the series MVP pitcher Mickey Lolich. The key play was a Billy Northrup triple that center fielder Curt Flood misplayed. It could have been the third out with no runs scored.

I have always had this tendency to be very loud, animated, and physical whenever watching a sporting event. The bigger the event, the bigger my emotional responses. Curt Flood misplayed a fly ball in the seventh inning, and immediately, I jumped into the air with my arms flailing aimlessly. I knocked over and broke one of my mother's table lamps. Mom watched as this entire mishap took place. Her reaction to my outburst came out sharp and loud. "Michael Anthony (she added my middle name when she was really upset with me), look what you've done!" she exclaimed. This was one of her favorite twin lamps, which had been in her possession for a long time.

I surveyed the broken lamp pieces spread out over the floor and reacted defensively with an excuse, "It is the dang Cardinal's fault. That outfielder of ours blew the play." The look on Mom's face told me this response was only making matters worse. Then, I meekly admitted responsibility for my actions. "I am sorry, Mom. I lost control of my emotions."

In one "fell swoop," all in the name of baseball and the St. Louis Cardinals, these two errors created insult to injury. Curt Flood's misplay of the ball was an insult to the Cardinals and may well have cost them a World Series. The injury was all those broken pieces lying on the floor from one of Mom's favorite lamps.

***

I had barely turned sixteen and could not wait to take the driver's test and get my license. I began my driver's test by displaying an air of confidence and cockiness. In hindsight, this was not the brightest move on my part. Halfway through my test, the examiner shut it down. I got quite frustrated and could not understand why this person would be stopping my perfect driving performance.

He then questioned me, "Do you know why I stopped your test?" Of course, I had no idea. The examiner had me driving through a subdivision of family homes where the speed limit sign read twenty-five mph. According to the examiner, my driving speed was around thirty miles per hour. It felt like I was crawling, so I never even thought to put my focus on it or check on the speedometer.

The examiner offered up a little bit of advice to me, "Son, come back after you get rid of your lead foot." I easily passed on the second try, closely watching my speed. It certainly did not hurt me to get a different driving examiner.

My first year of driving was a rough one. I had two fender benders and one bad accident. It is quite possible that the only thing I learned driving home late at night was basic driving skills. There was always little to no traffic on the road. Dad would always fall asleep on the ride, which made me think that I knew what I was doing. Of course, knowing basic driving skills alone does not make you a good or safe driver. It is the knowledge and understanding of what is going on around you while taking all the necessary precautions to drive defensively. This was the part of my driver's education that I ended up learning the hard way.

***

My sister, Lucia, believed that she had found the love of her life. This potential soon-to-be brother-in-law, Mike

Green, discovered this in an embarrassing and silly sort of way. His college degree was in engineering, and he was also particularly good at handyman-type jobs around the house. Whenever Mom invited him over for dinner, she would always find a home project for him. Mike was always willing and happy to comply with her request.

On this one night, she asked him to add another light fixture to a section of the basement that was dark. He did not want to cut off the power because Mom was baking her famous Christmas cookies. Lucia stood next to him, holding up a flashlight in the area where Mike was completing the necessary wiring.

My youngest brother, Rio, had decided to go downstairs and be a little pest. There is one thing you can always count on: this brother loves to shock people with his comments. He walked right up to them and proudly announced, "Hey Mike, my sister told me I better be good because you might be the one."

Within seconds, Lucia ran up the basement steps, leaving Mike holding live wires while standing on a chair in the dark. Upon reaching the family room, my sister dropped to her knees. Mom walked over to her and inquired, "What is the matter with you?" Lucia explained to her what had transpired, and while Mom was still laughing, she declared in the same breath, "I'm going to kill him!" Fortunately, everyone managed to survive that evening, and most importantly, Mike Green did not get scared away!

(The 9th Inning)

---1969---

My parents continued going through the same motions day in and day out, hoping this would be enough to continue holding onto their restaurant business. At the very least, they wanted to keep the business going until they completed all payments for ownership of the restaurant. If they kept bringing in their current sales, it might be possible to stay afloat and pull it off. It was important that they make every effort to fulfill their commitment. They had at least two years left of their contract with Phil Polizzi.

I continued working on the weekends and doing my part. If there was one regret, it was never having an opportunity to take over that massive barbeque pit and master the cooking of twenty or more slabs of ribs at one time. What I never regretted was those dreaded Monday night rides into town and mopping up all those floors in the restaurant.

My sister Lucia was right; Mike Green was "the one.' Mom had already begun making the necessary preparations for the wedding. She then learned that the guest list would be much smaller than anticipated, and most guests were from our side of the family. This meant our parents might be able to swing a reception party without the need to cater for it themselves. After finding a proper size banquet room large enough for the reception party, Mom began haggling over the pricing for 160 to 180 guests.

She finally got them to come down to an agreeable price, but the venue only served beer. Lucia had already seen how hard our parents worked during her first three sisters' weddings, and she wanted them to fully enjoy this one. "We don't need any other liquor; beer is enough," she argued. Mom and Dad talked it over and agreed to go ahead with this chosen reception hall at the offered price.

The wedding day began with the sun coming in and out, not too warm, considering it was the 31st of May. Everything was going well until it came time for the evening reception, and tornado siren warnings sounded out. As cars started pulling into the reception parking lot, wind, rain, and hail were coming down. Lucia's beautiful veil almost blew off her very coiffed hair as she made her way into the banquet hall.

Entering the room, you could hear half of the people talking in Italian and the other half in English, all of them without a worry whatsoever as to what was going on outside. Mom and Dad were finally able to fully celebrate their daughter's wedding reception. For once, they were having dinner served to them instead of cooking and serving all the guests. While dancing together, my family overheard friends and family comment on how happy and still in love our parents were with one another.

As they were leaving the reception, the bride and groom remarked on their wonderful evening. The night air smelled fresh as it sometimes does after a spring rain. Dad was so proud and thrilled to have been able to give his first four daughters a festive Italian wedding. This entailed a big church ceremony, a large reception consisting of family members and friends, substantial amounts of food, a music band, Italian cookies, and candy.

Being the proprietors of their own restaurant, my parents could afford to purchase food and do the catering for my first three sisters' weddings. This smaller reception now gave them an opportunity to pay for the catering and genuinely enjoy the event. Otherwise, they could not have given my sisters these beautiful and special weddings. If nothing else, they saw it as one good thing that came about in owning a family restaurant business.

Shortly after my sister Lucia's wedding day, Mom entered the hospital for a partial hysterectomy. This meant she would be out of commission for a while. Dad was stuck with having to open the restaurant in the morning and staying until closing. My school year had just ended, and I became the logical choice to help with the opening every day. This was not exactly the way I planned to start my summer vacation, and I can remember moping about the place, physically showing my desire not to be there.

By the third or fourth day, Dad had gotten his fill of my attitude. We had just finished grinding up a large piece of beef. All the ground beef lay inside this humongous stainless-steel bowl, big enough for three people to stand around. We took a portion of the ground beef and started making hamburgers. Another portion was set aside to make hamburger sausage for pizza toppings. The remaining ground beef would be used to make meatballs.

Our waitress, Mary, Dad, and I stood around this huge bowl with the remaining ground beef. We threw in other ingredients and spices inside the bowl. After mixing it all together, we began rolling out the leftover ground beef into meatballs. I was moving very slowly, expressing a look of real pity and sadness on my face.

This must have been the last straw as far as Dad was concerned. He proceeded to pick up a handful of raw ground beef and then flung it directly into my face. "I need you here with me right now, he barked at me, "Your mother is in the hospital, and you are standing there sulking."

I could tell that Mary was horrified and felt awful for me. "Vince, that's not right what you did," she remarked. Not just anyone could have gotten away with that kind of remark directed toward my dad. However, she was a long-time, loyal employee, and there was a tremendous amount of respect between the two of them.

This act of his was embarrassing, but it was also humiliating. For just a moment, I felt hatred in my heart for what he had done to me. Dad was under heavy pressure, and I understood that he was counting on Mary and me during this challenging time. My problem is he never thought about or took into consideration my feelings about having to be there. I began wondering if I could ever get over this unworthy and barbaric act. But then, good old unconditional love kicked in. This was the only way I felt that I could have ever allowed myself to forgive him completely.

Mom returned home from the hospital and came back to work in record-breaking time. She was not the type to stay laid up in bed, nor could she afford to be. I was incredibly grateful to get a little break from the grind of going into the restaurant every day.

It was not long after this when Dad received a disturbing phone call at our home in the middle of the night. "Vince, I had to call the fire department. Your restaurant is on fire." It came from Sonja, the woman who lived next store to our restaurant, along with her husband Vince, Phil Polizzi's son.

I was fast asleep and had no idea what happened. Upon his return home that day, Dad explained how someone had broken the main left window next to the entrance and tossed a firebomb into the place. Thanks to our neighbor Sonja acting quickly, the fire department arrived in time to save the place. However, there had been extensive damage to the inside of our restaurant.

The very next day, Dad began cleaning up the place. One of his first jobs was to properly board up the broken front window. Looking at it from my perspective, it seemed as if the restaurant had gotten a black eye. The two large picture windows on each side of the front door entrance appeared to me as the eyes of our place. One looked perfectly fine, but the other window had to be all boarded up. It was going to require a great amount of work, including quite a bit of interior painting, before the restaurant would be able to reopen.

That Sunday, my brothers and brothers-in-law came over to the restaurant to do whatever possible to help repair the damage. One of my brothers-in-law, Vince Monteleone, being an expert tailor, always came dressed in fine clothing. At the time, he did not even own casual or work clothes. When he entered the restaurant in dress clothes, all the others could not help laughing at his attire. They were all clothed in their worst garb. "Hey, Vince, did you come here to fit us for suits, or were you planning on doing some other work?" one of them teased.

After taking one look at the condition of our restaurant and the other men, Vince immediately surmised he came overdressed for this type of work. Fortunately, one of my other brothers-in-law had brought along spare clothes and saved the day. Although this was a somber occasion, his coming into the place all dressed up seemed to lighten the mood a bit.

Over the next couple of weeks, Dad, with help from my brother Nick, took care of the remaining portion of the needed repairs. From time to time, customers would come by only to find the restaurant closed. However, there were times when the front door would get left unlocked, and people would walk into the place. "We were firebombed," Dad would sometimes reply to the customer inquiries, but then quickly added, "but we expect to be up and running again very soon."

"Dad! Why are you telling customers about our place getting firebombed?" Nick inquired. "Tell them we are remodeling or painting the place due to a fire – anything other than we got firebombed." Although Dad was simply being honest, it was obvious he was not taking into consideration the ramifications of his words. Considering the changing make-up and current direction in which the neighborhood was heading, it seemed quite likely people hearing this kind of news might think twice before dining in or revisiting our place.

The most frustrating part of this entire tragedy was the fact we had no idea who or why someone would perform this malicious act. We did not have, nor did we know of any enemies or neighbors with bad feelings toward us. My parents racked their brains and made inquiries, trying to discover any reason for someone wishing to cause us harm.

There were different rumors bandied about, but then we heard of one specific and disturbing rumor. As I understood it, Phil Polizzi's son, Vince, the man who lived next store to our restaurant, had fired a gun at a stray dog in the neighborhood. He missed the dog, and the bullet ricocheted, hitting a utility worker and allegedly killing the man. The word on the street was Vince Polizzi might be facing manslaughter charges.

There were people still under the impression that Phil Polizzi had ties to the restaurant next door. For this very reason, there was speculation the firebombing may have been in retaliation. It meant that this attack may have come from someone with close ties to the deceased man.

The firebombing of our restaurant could eventually put an end to our business. It very well may have happened due to actions caused by the eldest son of the man who sold the place to us. Oh, the irony of it all. However, since the perpetrator got away, there was no proof of this being the reason for the fire-bombing.

After reopening, the restaurant closely resembled the same activity found in a ghost town. Mom and Dad were hoping that once our customers realized we were open for business, they would return. For now, our customer base seemed limited to people inside and around the neighborhood, yielding fewer and smaller total sales. Unfortunately, the restaurant would never return to the way it was before the firebombing.

***

Summer had come to its end, and I was back at high school for my junior year. Based on the amount of business at the restaurant, there was no longer a need for me to continue going there on weekends. In all his years at the restaurant, Dad never brought up or discussed any of the incidents that occurred. It was not, at least, until late one evening after closing.

There was no longer any reason to keep the restaurant open late at night. Dad got home one evening and proceeded to tell me about an incident with a Black man who had come into the restaurant earlier that day. Our waitress, Mary, caught this man trying to steal something. He reacted by showing unruly behavior toward her for stopping and accusing him of theft. Dad, hearing the commotion, spotted this man acting up and quickly confronted him. "Get the hell out of my place!" he ordered. The man replied, "Oh yeah, who's gonna make me?" He then continued ranting on. By this point, it became obvious this guy must be high on drugs.

Dad did not want any trouble with this man, but after all these years of frustration, he might have reached a breaking point. This person needed to be gone from his place. He attempted to scare him off by firing a gunshot over the man's head. The man quickly dropped to the floor with his eyes closed. He then began feeling all around his body, then opening his eyes, he popped back up from the ground. "You missed me; try again!" he sarcastically cried out. Dad must have given off one of his killing stares and responded, "One last time, get the hell out of my place."

All I know is this doped-up guy must have left because Dad was here to tell me the story. However, this made me even more anxious and worried that one of these times, something bad was going to happen. After this incident, along with the continued decline in business, Dad informed his waitress, "Mary, I will not be needing you to come in anymore. I can manage the business by myself."

It had been a year since the assassination of Martin Luther King Jr., but this feeling of disrespect continued to grow even stronger among the Black community. You could say there was a huge chip on their shoulder in trying to deal with these deep-rooted feelings of disrespect and racism. Consider all three of these incidents that occurred at our restaurant.

First, the two Black women felt the young punk on the phone was being disrespectful in using foul language in front of them. Second, there was the Black man whom Dad bumped into when coming out of the restroom. Although it may have been a matter of semantics with the English language, in getting a "pardon me" rather than "excuse me," this man might have felt disrespected. And lastly, the Black man whom our waitress Mary accused of trying to steal something. He also may have felt disrespected by the accusation of committing theft.

Over time, I have created a theory about all three of the confrontations that took place between my dad and these Black individuals. Admittedly, all three of these incidents were bizarre events. However, there is reason for me to believe they may have all occurred for the same reason. It is quite possible that in all three incidents, these individuals felt a lack of respect coming from the white race.

***

Over the next few weeks, Dad was the only person working at our restaurant. After Mom stopped going into the restaurant, she said to me, "He sits in the back section of that kitchen watching television all day long, waiting for customers to come in." I also knew Dad always kept a bottle of whiskey hidden in the back section of the kitchen. Every so often, I would see him taking a big swig right out of the bottle. I do not believe that he did this often. Usually, it occurred whenever he was feeling overly stressed, distraught, or concerned over a bigger problem that might be happening at the time. For that matter, he might be having a shot right then to ease the pain of his business, which is all but destroyed and coming to its end.

At this point, robberies were occurring in all the places of business within the surrounding neighborhood. It had gotten to the point where businesses were permanently shutting down. Yet through it all, there still had not been one robbery attempt at our place of business. There were a couple of times someone broke in after closing. They came in through one of the dining room windows, but there was no money inside for them to take. I suppose out of anger, they could have taken food or messed up and damaged the place, but it did not happen. That is, until someone decided to firebomb us.

Every night during those last few weeks, I feared for Dad's safety. I would imagine all types of potentially bad scenarios. I could only hope and pray that he would shut down the restaurant before something bad happened.

Over the past few months, my brother Mariano had asked Dad a couple of times to shut the place down. We were losing money, and it no longer made sense to keep the business going. Dad just could not allow himself to let go and admit defeat. My continuous fear of someone robbing us, thankfully, never did happen. To my way of thinking, there was only one ultimate explanation - divine intervention. I do not want to imagine or care to think how things might have turned out if a robbery attempt had ever taken place.

The end of the year was approaching fast. Dad finally accepted the inevitable decision to permanently shut down the restaurant. He would have to make an extremely difficult visit to speak with Phil Polizzi, "It is over. There is nothing more I can do to keep the place going," he explained. Dad took the keys to the restaurant and handed them over to Phil. "I have no other choice. All I can do is surrender the place back over to you," he sadly admitted. It was not the ending either one of these men wanted. Phil may have decided to accept the terms and restaurant back from Dad, as it might have been better than getting nothing.

Based on the amount of business coming through the door, there was no other choice. It was extremely painful for Dad to accept and realize he could not hold onto this place long enough to pay it off and then try to sell it himself. Instead, he could do nothing other than surrender the place back to Phil, adding insult to humiliation.

There is no way of knowing what Phil Polizzi received in the reselling of this property. It was around a year or two before I found an opportunity to take a sentimental drive late one night past the old place. The little brick and stone building on the corner of Elliott & Sullivan was gone, and this piece of history became a parking lot.

***

My family has survived and gone through a variety of turbulent and challenging times throughout our lives, and the 1960s were no different. As for me, I will always have memories of my time on the corner of Elliott and Sullivan. Also, I shared a special relationship with my dad through all those years. I cannot help but admire the way my parents faced, dealt with, and overcame one adversity after another, day after day. I was proud to stand alongside them, trying to make a go of this restaurant that had already seen its better days. For me, it was an awkward time in a special place. Thus, it became one of the most impactful periods of my lifetime.

In relating all these tales and reflecting upon my various memories, one question kept troubling me. Why is it that I can vividly recall so many memories relating to life's difficulties, regrets, sadness, embarrassment, ignorance, and despair? What about all the countless joyful, exciting, happy, loving, and more successful moments in my time?

I have come to believe, for different and distinct reasons, that there are specific events in our lives that subconsciously stay locked inside our minds that we are not allowed to escape. Every so often, these memories try to escape, and they resurface. Each time it attempts to escape, we stop it. At the same time, we give ourselves a chance to reflect on it with a different feeling or opinion about that memory.

There may even come a point in time when something happens to affect the way we may now feel about the entire memory or event. And who knows, the day may come when you will set it free from yourself. I ask myself, is it possible that this is part of the process which has created such powerful and vivid memories of my past?

I believe all the wonderful daily events occurring in our lives, which we take for granted, permeate throughout our body and soul. There is no purpose or reason for them to become trapped inside our minds. These things are what we freely and willingly release into the universe of God's love. They burst from our body and soul through the emotions of a smile, a laugh, a tear of joy, a cry of excitement, happiness, or a feeling of love.

I am certain we have all heard this phrase more than once in our lives: "Baseball is the Great American Pastime." For me, all those years growing up around my family and the special years spent with my dad at our restaurant became "An Unforgettable Past Time." There is also this funny little saying, which, from my point of view, I considered to be a prophetic statement, "Baseball is Life." It certainly seems to have become a part of mine and has also played a role in my life.

It began with those times spent with Dad at the parking lot during St. Louis Cardinals' ball games. I sat in the parking lot with Dad and my brothers, listening to ball games over the car radio. Our family restaurant is only three blocks from Busch Stadium and my walks down Sullivan Street to watch a Cardinals' ball game. The feeling of knowing baseball was in the air whenever a game was played at Busch Stadium while I worked at the restaurant. All those weeks in the summertime that I spent with my cousins playing diverse types of ball games, whether it be in or outside their house. And to top it all off, when the Cardinals moved their home away from our restaurant, I found myself taking on the role of working at the new ballpark.

I have taken into consideration the various disappointments resulting from my relationship with baseball. The one time I got myself involved in playing organized baseball, I took a hit to my mouth with a baseball and later nearly choked to death. Getting an autographed baseball hand-signed by every St. Louis Cardinal player only to be devastated by foolishly and literally throwing it down the sewer? All my valuable and timeless baseball player cards that I worked so hard to save and accumulate, only to be heartbroken after discovering they were gone forever due to mom's clutter-free and cleanliness habits. Watching the Cardinals on the verge of a World Series throw it away on a bad play and causing me to break one of Mom's favorite lamps.

I also wondered and contemplated two of the saddest and most tragic events that happened during my attendance at Cardinals' ballgames: First, celebrating a winning victory and returning to the restaurant only to hear my grandmother had passed away. Then, almost 25 years later, I lived through an almost identical experience to discover my mother had passed away.

After careful analysis, I came to discover something quite remarkable. Yes, it is quite possible I could have easily felt resentment and disdain by the outcome of these awful circumstances, all related and tied to baseball. After careful study, I came to this amazing realization and conclusion that all these misfortunes have never affected my love, respect, or admiration for baseball.

Taking this a step further, I began considering what my parents could have done differently or better. Discussions and other things that might have protected my siblings and me from living through certain disappointments, embarrassments, burdens, distraught, despair, hardships, troubling times, or other stupid and ignorant acts. I find myself coming to the same realization and conclusion: None of these things ever affected the love, respect, and admiration we had for our parents.

"Aha," I thought to myself. "What about my siblings and certain disappointments, distraught, despair, embarrassments, and unhappiness we caused our parents through all our actions and decisions? For that matter, what about the hardships, troubling times, and an enormous amount of demanding work our parents endured for our sake? Again, I came to the same realization and conclusion that through it all, none of it ever affected their love, respect, and admiration for us, their children.

Wait a minute! What about the mistreatment, destruction, greed, harm, and sins we have done to our fellow man that our Heavenly Father has endured from his children, his very creation? Again, I produce the same realization and conclusion: this will never affect his love for us.

Finally, I asked myself, "Should not God, our Creator, be given this same love from all of us?" Everything and anything that comes our way in a lifetime should never affect the love, respect, and admiration we have for the Lord God Almighty, our Creator.

(Extra Innings)

---1970 and Beyond---

There was "no quit" in Dad or Mom. A brief time after the closure of Elliott & Sullivan, they went back into the restaurant business. They were able to do this with the financial backing of my brother, Mariano. Around this same time, Dad met up with a former co-worker, Matt Slezak, from his days at Hostess Cake. He was currently managing a large Wonder Bread/Hostess Cake depot, and Matt offered him a job there.

Dad was over 60 years old and working the maintenance job at the depot by day and his restaurant business in the evening. After the shutting down of his last restaurant, he continued doing his day job. It turned out to be a comfortable, easy workplace until his retirement.

In the fall of 1970, I entered my senior year of high school. I wanted to find part-time work and make a bit of money. Dad had my back on this one and went along with me to a nearby IHOP (International House of Pancakes). He spoke with the owner and bragged about my cooking talents at the restaurant. The owner hired me on the spot. I was only seventeen years old, and boys my age could only get the position of dishwasher or busser. However, the IHOP owner hired me for a position in the kitchen galley as a short-order cook.

Two cooks from the galley overheard this news, and I noticed one of them pointing his spatula at me. "Him, they hired him to cook?" he retorted. They seemed miffed by the owner choosing someone my age for the job. It was certainly an adjustment from my days working at my restaurant. However, I proved my skills and capabilities for doing the job with a fair amount of ease in a brief period.

In hindsight, it seems to me the owner had ulterior motives in making his decision to hire me. All the older cooks made somewhere between two and three dollars per hour. My pay was a dollar fifty an hour, a quarter more than the dishwashers and bussers. After a couple of months, I received a quarter raise. A couple of the more ambitious bussers wanted to try for the job of a short-order cook. Since I was doing a very creditable job, the owner decided, why not? Eventually, we started training a couple of the bussers and dishwashers to be cooks.

I gave a portion of my salary to Dad, just as everyone else in the family had done when they first started working. After graduating from high school, I worked at IHOP full-time through the summer. All the money I saved went to pay for junior college. After the first semester of junior college, I quit IHOP and went to work part-time at the Army Records Center in St. Louis.

It was at this new workplace my supervisor introduced me to horse racing and the art of handicapping races. I continued my college education for a while, but my focus was not on my studies, and eventually, I dropped out of junior college. Shortly thereafter, the Army Records Center caught fire in July 1973, and I awoke one morning to discover myself out of work. I took a job at this loud, stinky, and greasy factory where they manufactured metal casings for electrical wiring. Thankfully, this job only lasted for a brief time.

Next, I got a job working at my dad's truck depot, loading Hostess Cake and Wonderbread products onto delivery trucks. The work schedule required me to work overnight and into the morning. This is where one of the night employees introduced me to smoking marijuana.

At this point, I had become involved in sports betting, horse race handicapping, and smoking marijuana. On the weekends, I added drinking and partying to the mix. This put me in a sustained trance that kept me working at the truck depot for seven years. I continued with my task of loading bread and cake trucks late at night and into the morning. Eventually, I came to my senses, realizing this was not the place to spend the rest of my life.

At the start of 1981, I landed an entry-level position with A. G. Edwards & Sons, a stock brokerage firm. At this job, my starting salary was about half of my salary for loading trucks. However, it allowed me to work in a clean office environment and develop better social skillsets with future job growth opportunities. Of course, this position did nothing to prevent me from the continuance of my vices.

***

After graduating from high school, my younger sister, Maria, went to work just as Dad expected her to do. After working for about a year or so, she realized this current job was never going to help fulfill her greater ambitions. Maria then showed real toughness and courage by standing up to Mom and Dad, refusing to follow the path of her four older sisters. She made up her mind to pursue higher education, and under no terms would that change. Maria received her B.A. in political science; however, this was only the first step toward a future goal.

Moving out of our parents' home, she soon returned to school and graduated from St. Louis University's School of Law. After passing the Missouri Bar exam, she would later get her career off the ground at the public defender's office for the state of Missouri. In 1981, she married the love of her life, a colleague and professional attorney, Marty Perron.

***

Mariano finally ventured out on his own, attempting to build a more fulfilling life for himself. He lived and worked in the cities of Washington, D.C., Atlanta, Georgia, and Tampa, Florida. During this time, a week did not go by without him calling one or more siblings to check on how they were doing. He always came home to visit once or twice a year, and we would take turns going down there to visit with him.

After retirement, Mom and Dad moved into a new home built on a three-acre plot of ground. My brother, Mariano, continued the never-ending financial support of our parents. This allowed all of us other siblings to be financially unencumbered and free to pursue our own financial goals and dreams.

My brother, Nick, working along with two other men, was handed the task of completing the prefabricated house our parents had selected. Prefabricated, or "prefab" homes, get manufactured piece by piece in an off-site factory, then transported to the home site and assembled on the homeowner's property. Dad could not stop himself from getting involved and pitching in to get the house completed. During his retirement years in this home, he cherished and flourished every day by basking in the joy of growing and admiring his large vegetable and fruit garden. He continuously added more trees to the property, including a variety of fruit trees.

Retirement allowed our parents to spend more time with all of us. My siblings would all take turns coming to visit. Our parents never knew for sure which ones were going to show up at every big Sunday afternoon get-together, and to them, the more, the merrier. Never did a weekend go by without, at the least, a couple of them coming over and bringing along the grandchildren.

There were no dogs around to enjoy after the closing of our barbeque restaurant. So, Dad jumped at the opportunity of bringing them back into his life. Sheena was a beautiful light brown, short-haired mutt with unusually long eyelashes. Later, she gave birth to a single puppy who turned out to be pure black. We called him Jack, short for Blackjack. Throughout the day, Jack and Sheena would follow Dad around the entire day while he vigorously worked on the grounds and garden. His whole life was going about doing good old-fashioned hard physical work, and that was never going to change.

Mom continued to do what she had been doing throughout much of her life: taking care of her husband and children. That was because my younger brother Rio and I were still living at home. The two of us worked and drove together for the next four to five years at the same financial institution.

Mom loved working every weekday at the local high school cafeteria and told me, "I have so much fun at the school, and I love serving and talking to the young girls and boys. The cafeteria ladies are fun to work with, too." I am certain they all felt the same way because that is just who she happened to be.

***

It was now my youngest brother Rio's turn to get married to the love of his life, Marianne Santangelo. This would leave me as the lone child at home with both parents. I will never forget the night of my younger brother's wedding. I had been dealing with one of my horrible sinus infections and left the wedding a little early. Driving up the long driveway of my parent's home, I heard and still relive the infamous "Denkinger Call." His full name was Don Denkinger, the first base umpire in Game 6 of the 1985 World Series.

The St. Louis Cardinals were leading the Kansas City Royals three games to two. In the sixth game of the World Series, they took a 1–0 lead into the bottom of the ninth inning. The Cardinals took the field with a ninth-inning lead into ninety-seven games in the 1985 season and went on to win all ninety-seven times.

By a twist of fate, the streak would end on this night. In the bottom of the ninth, Jorge Orta, the leadoff batter for the Royals, hit a slow ground ball to first baseman Jack Clark. He tossed the ball to the pitcher, Todd Worrell, who was covering the first base bag. Denkinger called Orta safe, even though television replays (not used by officials for play review until 2008) and photographs clearly showed that he was out by half a step.

The Royals went on to win Game 6 by the score of 2–1. Baseball fate had once again dealt the St. Louis Cardinals and me a terrible blow. This quickly brought my hopes and expectations of another World Series down to earth. The next evening, the Cardinals went on to lose Game 7 and the World Series by an embarrassing score of 11-0.

The previous evening may have been one of the Cardinal's darkest days in its history. For my brother, Rio, it was his wedding and one of the brightest days of his life. So, there is no way I would ever consider or be willing to trade or exchange that day for his sake alone.

***

Two years after my youngest brother's wedding, my family celebrated our parents' 50th wedding anniversary. We rented out a large reception hall and invited relatives and friends to help celebrate this momentous occasion. All of us children got together and gifted them a two-week vacation for their first time to Rome, Italy, and then down to Sicily. On this trip, they got an opportunity to visit the area where Dad's parents were born. As they departed for their overseas adventure, my responsibility was to watch carefully over the house and our two dogs.

Everything went great during that first week. By the second week, our two dogs were badly missing their master. The dogs were not getting enough of my attention to fulfill their needs. I could see this myself. However, work and doing other things were taking priority over them.

I then proceeded to get home extremely late one night due to playing in a company department ball game. This meant the dogs had to wait a long time for their daily feeding. After putting out their food inside the garage, I walked down to the backyard and let them out to be fed. Instead of heading into the garage, they took off running. I had a bit too much to drink, and this was not the first time they had run off. I figured since they had been stuck in the backyard all week, they needed a little freedom to roam around. After getting a nice run out of their system, they would be back within hours, eat their food, and head back down into the yard. As for myself, I was going straight to bed.

Getting up the next morning, I headed out for work but noticed the dogs had not yet returned. That evening, there was still no sign of the dogs, and I started to panic. The next morning, they still had not returned. I knew that a plan of action was going to be necessary to find them. I could not bear the thought of my parents coming home from Sicily and finding our dogs had gone missing under my watch.

I was upset and frustrated and could not even think about going to work the following day. My sister, Catherine, had the idea of placing an ad about our lost dogs in the local newspaper. One of my brothers-in-law, Mike Green, came over to help me try to locate the dogs. We drove all around the area but stayed within close range of our house. As we drove around, he informed me, "Generally, when a dog runs off, it will always stay within a two-mile radius of their home." Unfortunately, we had no luck in locating them, and things began to look bleaker with each passing moment.

I was becoming sick with grief and distraught over losing those dogs. I had no idea what to do, nor could I imagine facing my dad and confessing this news. I prayed, begged, and cried for the Lord to bring these dogs somehow back to me.

It was only a couple of days before my parents were to arrive back home when I got a call from my sister, Catherine, "I received this phone call from a man who said that he saw two dogs matching my description in the newspaper. He spotted them somewhere along the intersection of Highway T and Highway 100," she said. This was less than two miles from our home. However, my pessimistic attitude discounted it and sorely replied. "I have already gone over and through that area."

Then came Saturday, the day before our parents were to arrive home. I had given up all hope, still unsure as to how I was going to face my father and deliver the news. Catherine called me again and insisted that I pick her up, and we went out looking again. She then said to me, "I don't know how to explain it, but when I heard that man's voice telling me where he spotted the dogs, it sounded and felt like the voice of an angel."

We drove around the area in question but found and saw nothing. Catherine spotted a dirt road jutting out from a heavily wooded area near the intersection of Highway 100 near Highway T. "Turn your car onto this dirt road," she instructed me. We took a steep dive to the bottom of this road and discovered there were houses under construction.

It was Saturday morning, so there were no workers or any activity. After driving up and down the road, I prepared to make my way out of there. Another car was coming down the road, and after passing us by, they pulled up to one of the houses under construction. As they were getting out of their car, we could see it was a family with two small children. This family must have decided to come and check on the progress of their new home.

Suddenly, from out of the woods, we spotted two dogs running toward the family. The commotion from getting out of their car must have drawn the attention of these dogs. My heart leaped, "Oh my God," I said. "It's Jack and Brownie."

We raced our way over to the house while this family stood watching our two dogs excitedly wagging their tails at them. I jumped out of the car, running and grabbing hold of both dogs. One at a time, I picked up these two huge animals and carried them back to my car. Somehow, I managed to fit them both in the back seat. This family just stood there watching everything happening in front of them and looking quite dumbfounded. I have never felt a bigger load come off my shoulders than at that exact moment. The next day, my parents arrived home, and our dogs were back in the yard. Everything was right in my world for another day.

***

Time was running out on me, and I needed to act now if I was ever going to achieve a more favorable and normal lifestyle. I had been living this vicarious life and doing whatever suited or pleased me. Sometimes, Mom would say to me, "Where are you going?" and my answer was always, "Wherever the wind takes me."

My favorite vices, betting on horses and other sports, smoking marijuana, and social drinking all worked at keeping me stuck in an unsavory lifestyle. Understand that I was having fun, enjoyment, and excitement, living this type of lifestyle. The thing was, a gambler's money has no home, and getting high on marijuana was doing nothing to help me get anywhere in life. I did my best to keep this part of my life a secret from my parents. However, they knew whatever I was doing was not a good thing. They were always attempting to nudge me in a better direction but never in a forceful way. My parents enabled and supported me, all the while keeping the faith and hoping that one day, I would turn my life around.

It was impossible for me to overlook the remarkable examples my parents and all my siblings had shown me in the way they were living their lives. This embarrassed me to the point of pushing myself to take the higher road in life. The first step in finally taking responsibility for myself was being on my own. I pushed myself to find and move into a one-bedroom apartment.

Mom passed away in 1990. It was less than a year after I had finally moved out of the house. I could not imagine leaving Dad alone in that empty house or seeing him do all that well after all those years being with Mom. So, I decided to move back home.

If there was only one thing that I could say about my mother, it would be about all the people who loved and appreciated her. The biggest testament to this fact happened right after her death. Her funeral included two full days of visitation. I was amazed and startled by the hundreds of people who came through to see her one last time, and I had absolutely no idea she had touched the lives of so many people.

In the telling of this story, Dad became a major focus, in part due to our deep relationship built in working and being together. I have come to develop a great appreciation for his devotion and dedication to family. Wrongfully, I always took everything my mother did for granted and simply expected her to sacrifice. We were the one true family that belonged solely to her, and this is what she cared most about her children.

Dad tried his best to move on by taking up additional projects and hobbies to stay busy. He came upon this one hobby where he put significant effort into buying different molds and a kiln oven to make all types of ceramic statues. One thing he thoroughly enjoyed doing was decorating the molds with all types of paint finishes. His favorite project of all was to create a complete sixteen-piece nativity scene for every one of his children. Each one of my siblings received a uniquely painted version of these nativity molds. Dad struggled to do as best he could without Mom in those remaining seven years.

Living for six months alone with Dad further magnified my understanding and my need to make a change in my life path. I met Debbie Muench for the very first time at St. Louis Cardinal's Hall of Famer Ozzie Smith's Restaurant and Sports Bar. Once again, baseball managed a subtle way of presenting itself in my life. My sister, Catherine, and Debbie's mom had been trying for years to get us together. It turned into a whirlwind romance that I felt was going to require a specially written proposal of marriage to seal the deal.

At the time, one of my all-time favorite rock groups was "The Doors," and this was my opening in managing to produce my written marriage proposal.

I have been through my share of doors. My favorite doors are the ones that I find my family behind. So, you would tend to think I am a family man, but on my way to the right door, I lost my way.

When I met you, it opened a new and different door for me. It was a door with a different kind of love filled with happiness, warmth, and care. I do not believe I have ever gone through this one door before, and now I am discovering this door opens too many other doors which I have never seen before.

What I am trying to say is I can see my life expanding with you. I have been living a one-room life. I want to live a home life, a real life, and you are the girl for me to live

We were married on December 14, 1991, and later blessed with two children, Meredith and Vincent. Dad was quite insistent that none of the grandchildren take his name. Somehow, he had come to this belief that his name was unlucky. Debbie had already made up her mind and refused to adhere to his nonsense. In the end, he could not have been happier or prouder when my son was born and named after him. Vince Damiano Vitale was the last grandchild born into his family.

After marriage, I went back to weekend college and graduated with a bachelor's degree in business and accounting. Then, later, moved my family for two stays in Richmond, Virginia, and one in Boston, Massachusetts. There, I continued to progress in my new career by working in compliance for Wachovia Securities, eventually earning the title of Vice President.

In 2008, we miraculously relocated back to our hometown of St. Louis after my company bought out my old firm, A. G. Edwards & Sons. It felt amazing to return home and work in the same building complex where I first started my business career in 1981. This is what you call going full circle.

***

My parents' commitment, hard work, and efforts in their barbecue and restaurant businesses never developed or reached the heights of the so-called "Great American Dream." Instead, what my parents did achieve was the "Greatest of All Dreams," their life purpose and legacy were all about their ten children. Everything they did in their life was for their children. It truly became their pride and joy to raise and instill faith, love,

221

and devotion in us. I believe it has been nothing short of a miracle to see how wonderful our lives have turned out over the past fifty years and beyond. God's love is capable of being as strong as you need it to be.

This steadfast faith, love, strength, toughness, resilience, and togetherness exemplified by our parents have served us all well. I am happy and proud that my family is an example of what you can achieve from the practice of these traits. We have all become outstanding citizens of our country. All the while living clean, God-fearing, successful lives. There is no doubt this will be handed down for generations to come.

(Team Celebration)

---Epilogue---

The life stories of my family continue to amaze me to this day. I would be remiss not to celebrate a brief history of our past fifty-plus years.

The first child - Don, resides in Bowling Green, Kentucky, and has lived there since the early 1980s. He has three children with his former wife, Suzanne. Their son, Robert, lives in St. Louis. Michael and Mary also live in Bowling Green.

Don's career first took his family to Minnesota, then the Philippines, Brazil, and finally to his current residence in Bowling Green, Kentucky. This is where he became part owner of an extraordinarily successful company. He went on to form Manchester Capital, a private investment company that he has managed for over 20 years.

Currently, Don is enjoying retirement with his companion, Linda. They love entertaining and being with friends. Their travels include visits to their condominium in Naples, Florida. Don enjoys spending time with his six grandchildren and has recently become a great-grandfather. He also enjoys taking trips to St Louis, visiting with other siblings and his eldest son, Robert.

The second child – Mariano, passed away in 2017 and joined our parents in the heavenly kingdom of our Lord Savior, Jesus Christ.

His commitment to family was unending. He never married but was always there for Mom, Dad, his siblings, nieces, and nephews. He touched, influenced, and supported us to the point of financially helping in times of need, expecting nothing in return.

He was an avid reader throughout his life, possessing a wealth of knowledge. After leaving St. Louis, his career took him to the DC area, Atlanta, and Tampa. He spent his final years in St. Louis, where hardly a day passed that he did not receive an open invitation from one of his siblings for dinner. Before he passed on, all nine of us were there for him. I can only hope this wonderful man felt the amount of love we had for him.

The third child – Patricia, and her husband, Steve Letko, have been married for 60 years, and they have resided in Atlanta for the past 40 years. Their son, Richard, lives in Indianapolis, and their daughter, Denise, lives in Williamsburg, Virginia.

In the early days, Steve spent a great deal of time working and attending St. Louis University. Patricia never complained about the time he would be gone or spent devoted to his studies. After receiving a master's degree in business, Crane Company offered him a job in California and eventually promoted him to Regional Sales Manager. After six years, they moved to Atlanta, and Steve became a partner at Dodson Steel Co.

Patricia has always been an incredibly supportive wife running the household, entertaining his business associates, and going with him on business travels, even to this day. Steve is now semi-retired, but they are still always on the go. They enjoy traveling and visiting their two children, five grandchildren, friends, and their families in St. Louis.

The fourth child – Catherine and her husband, Dennis Maxwell, have been married for 50-plus years and blessed with two children. Dennis started his career as an independent insurance agent and later added the title of Investment Advisor. Later in life, Catherine began assisting in his insurance and investment business.

Their son, Ray, and daughter, Mary, also live in St. Louis. As they aged into their mid-seventies, they had given up hope of becoming grandparents, but their son, Ray, surprised them with twins who light up their lives. They have retired and enjoy visiting their two children, twin grandchildren, other family, and friends.

The fifth child – Nick and his wife Joan, have been married for 50-plus years and blessed with two children, Lisa and Mark, along with one grandchild. Nick spent his early married life in the Insurance business. Later, he started running his own home improvement and repairs business. An injury on the job, along with the continued escalation of his multiple sclerosis, eventually forced him into early retirement.

After their children had grown, Joan took the opportunity to go back to work, helping to improve their financial future. They are now both retired and spend their time together enjoying their two children, grandchild, other family, and friends.

The sixth child – Theresa and her husband Vince Monteleone, have been married for 50-plus years and blessed with two children, Joe and Rose, along with six grandchildren. Vince, an expert tailor, eventually became the owner of his own Fine Tailoring shop. His tailoring services were in great demand and highly sought after. Thus creating a business of elite, influential customers and good friends.

Theresa took charge of all the financial and family matters, including management of their tailor shop business. This allowed Vince to focus his time and energy on tailoring and his customers' needs. Throughout their marriage, they have been involved with different Italian organizations and charities. They are both retired and spend their time together visiting with their two children, six grandchildren, other family, and friends.

The seventh child – Lucia, and her husband, Mike Green, have been married for 50-plus years and reside in the St. Louis area. Their two sons, Dan and Jason, also live in St. Louis. Over 45 years ago, they started up their company, Connectronics, from inside their home. They later began specializing in the designing and making of custom-built cables. This eventually allowed them to grow their customer base. After more than ten years of working and building up their business, they were able to lease out a large manufacturing building and continue the growth of their business.

Throughout the years, they have taken time to enjoy boating, taking their motor yacht up to Canada and down to Florida, with other enjoyable stops along the way. They have now retired and spend part of their time traveling and visiting with their three grandchildren, other family, and friends.

The eighth child – I have been married to Debbie for over 30 years. We are now retired and living in a 55-plus community called On Top of the World in Ocala, Florida. We enjoy going around in our golf cart and participating in activities inside the community.

You already know my early story. I spent almost 40 years in the securities industry. I have always wanted to be a published author, and now it has finally come to fruition.

Our son, Vince, lives in Denver, and our daughter, Meredith, lives in Nashville. Meredith is engaged, and they are planning a wedding in late 2024. We enjoy having our family come to visit our home. A great deal of our travels is visiting with our two children, other family, and friends.

The ninth child – Maria and her husband, Marty Perron, have been married for over 40 years and reside in St. Louis. Blessed with three children: David lives in St. Louis, Justin in Connecticut, and Rachel in Chicago.

Maria and Marty worked in the law profession and eventually started up their own successful law practice. They recently ended their practice. In retirement, they enjoy travel and spending time with their children, three grandchildren (one on the way), other family, and friends.

The tenth child – Rio, and his spouse, Marianna, have been married for over 35 years and live in St. Louis. Blessed with three children. Marissa and Matthew both live in St. Louis, and Andrew lives in Austin, Texas. Rio's career was in the securities industry, and he was instrumental in the growth of a startup online St. Louis stock brokerage firm, Scottsdale Securities.

Although retired, Rio's accomplishments continue to grow. In his early fifties, he decided to get more in touch with his family heritage and became involved with Italian organizations and charities. He has received the special honor and title of "Cavalier" from the Italian government.

His recent endeavor was producing two award-winning documentaries, "America's Last Little Italy - The Hill" and "A New Home," with a third documentary in the works. Rio and Marianna love to travel all over the world, especially Sicily and Hawaii. Most importantly, they enjoy being with their children, five grandchildren, other family, and friends.

Top Row, left to right

Don, Mariano, Michael,Nick

Bottom Row, left to right

Maria, Lucia. Dad, Rio, Mom, Theresa. Patricia. Catherine

Vincent and Lena Vitale

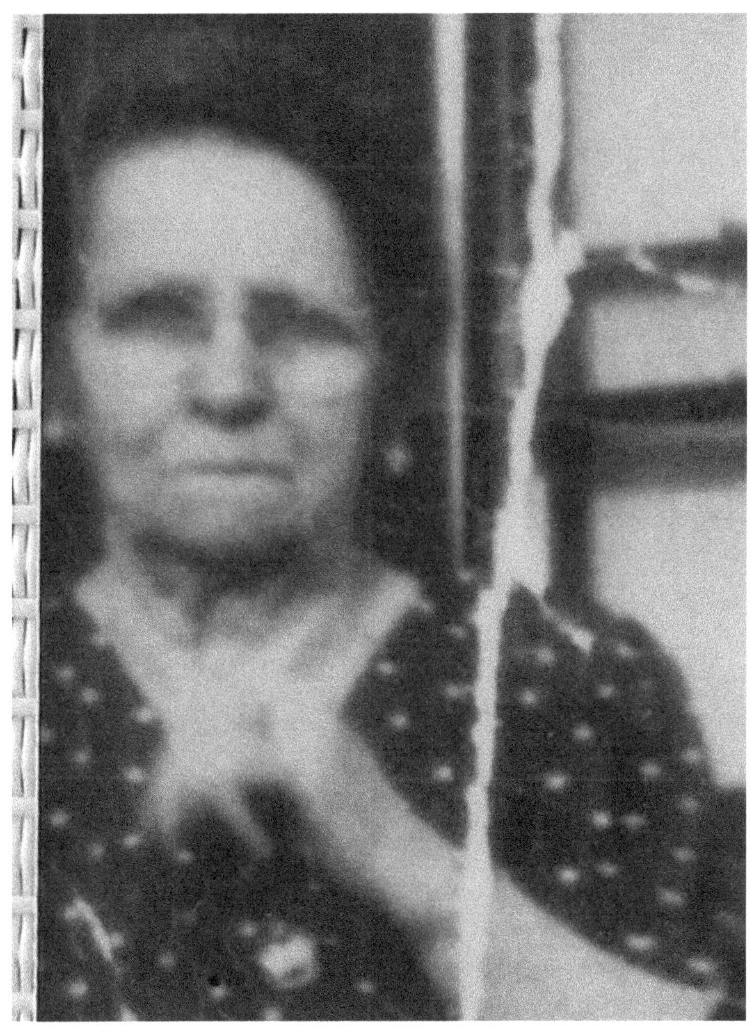

Catherine Deluca

Mariano DeLuca

Domiano and Patrina Vitale